Learning C++ Functional Programming

Metaprogramming, concurrency, lazy evaluation, and more

Wisnu Anggoro

BIRMINGHAM - MUMBAI

Learning C++ Functional Programming

First published: August 2017

Production reference: 1080817

Published by Packt Publishing Ltd.
Livery Place
35 Livery Street
Birmingham
B3 2PB, UK.

ISBN 978-1-78728-197-4

www.packtpub.com

Credits

Author
Wisnu Anggoro

Reviewer
Aivars Kalvāns

Commissioning Editor
Aaron Lazar

Acquisition Editor
Chaitanya Nair

Content Development Editor
Lawrence Veigas

Technical Editor
Supriya Thabe

Copy Editor
Zainab Bootwala

Project Coordinator
Prajakta Naik

Proofreader
Safis Editing

Indexer
Rekha Nair

Graphics
Abhinash Sahu

Production Coordinator
Nilesh Mohite

About the Author

Wisnu Anggoro is a Microsoft Certified Professional in C# programming and an experienced C/C++ developer. He has also authored the books *Boost.Asio C++ Network Programming - Second Edition* and *Functional C#* by Packt. He has been programming since he was in junior high school, which was about 20 years ago, and started developing computer applications using the BASIC programming language in the MS-DOS environment. He has solid experience in smart card programming, as well as desktop and web application programming, including designing, developing, and supporting the use of applications for SIM Card Operating System Porting, personalization, PC/SC communication, and other smart card applications that require the use of C# and C/C++. He is currently a senior smart card software engineer at CIPTA, an Indonesian company that specializes in innovation and technology for smart cards. He can be reached through his email at `wisnu@anggoro.net`.

First and foremost, I would like to thank God, the almighty, for providing me with this opportunity and granting me the capability to proceed successfully. To my wife and best motivator, Vivin, who never stopped supporting me in finishing what I started. To my beloved sons, Olav and Oliver, who are the source of my joy; you both never fail to make me happy every day. And to my parents and family for their inspiration.

The best team at PACKT, especially Lawrence Veigas, my content development editor, for his effort to help me supply the best content for this book, and Denim Pinto, who invited me to author this book.

Also, I would like to show my gratitude to Benediktus Dwi Desiyanto, my best mentor, teacher, and superior at CIPTA, who always supports me to leverage my skill set, for both hard and soft skills. And to all my friends at CIPTA, for the insight of C++ and functional programming I have learned from all of you.

About the Reviewer

Aivars Kalvāns holds the position of Lead Software Architect at Tieto Latvia. He has been working on the Card Suite payment card system for more than 15 years and maintains many core C++ libraries and programs. He is also responsible for the C++ programming guidelines, secure coding training, and code reviews, and he organizes and speaks at internal C++ developer meetups as well.

I would like to thank my lovely wife, Anete, and sons, Kārlis, Gustavs, and Leo, for making life much more interesting.

www.PacktPub.com

For support files and downloads related to your book, please visit `www.PacktPub.com`.

Did you know that Packt offers eBook versions of every book published, with PDF and ePub files available? You can upgrade to the eBook version at `www.PacktPub.com` and as a print book customer, you are entitled to a discount on the eBook copy. Get in touch with us at `service@packtpub.com` for more details.

At `www.PacktPub.com`, you can also read a collection of free technical articles, sign up for a range of free newsletters and receive exclusive discounts and offers on Packt books and eBooks.

`https://www.packtpub.com/mapt`

Get the most in-demand software skills with Mapt. Mapt gives you full access to all Packt books and video courses, as well as industry-leading tools to help you plan your personal development and advance your career.

Why subscribe?

- Fully searchable across every book published by Packt
- Copy and paste, print, and bookmark content
- On demand and accessible via a web browser

Customer Feedback

Thanks for purchasing this Packt book. At Packt, quality is at the heart of our editorial process. To help us improve, please leave us an honest review on this book's Amazon page at `https://www.amazon.com/dp/1787281973`.

If you'd like to join our team of regular reviewers, you can e-mail us at `customerreviews@packtpub.com`. We award our regular reviewers with free eBooks and videos in exchange for their valuable feedback. Help us be relentless in improving our products!

Table of Contents

Preface

Functional programming is a style of constructing the elements and structure of a computer program by composing pure functions, avoiding shared state, mutable data, and side-effects, like we usually see in mathematics. The variable in the code function represents the value of the function parameter, and it is similar to the mathematical function. The idea is that a programmer defines the functions that contain the expression, definition, and the parameters that can be expressed by a variable to solve problems.

Functional programming is declarative rather than imperative, which means programming is done with expressions or declarations instead of statements. The application state of functional programming flows through pure functions, so it avoids the side effect. In contrast to imperative programming, the application state is usually shared and collocated with methods in objects. In imperative programming, the expressions are evaluated, and the resulting value is assigned to variables. For instance, when we group a series of expressions into a function, the resulting value depends upon the state of variables at that point in time. Because of the continuous changes in state, the order of evaluation matters. In functional programming, destructive assignment is forbidden, and each time an assignment happens, a new variable is induced. Best of all, functional code tends to be more concise and predictable, and easier to test than imperative or object-oriented code.

Although there are some specifically designed languages for functional programming, such as Haskell and Scala, we can also use C++ to accomplish designing functional programming, as we will discuss throughout this book.

What this book covers

Chapter 1, *Diving into Modern C++*, provides an overview of modern C++, including the implementation of several new features in modern C++, such as the auto keyword, decltype keyword, null pointer, range-based for loop, standard template library, Lambda expressions, smart pointer, and tuple.

Chapter 2, *Manipulating Functions in Functional Programming*, covers the essential techniques in functional programming to manipulate a function; they are the first-class function technique, pure function, and currying technique. By applying the first-class function, we can treat our function as a data, which means it can be assigned to any variable instead of only being invoked as function. We also will apply the pure function technique so the function won't produce the side effect anymore. Moreover, to simplify the function, we can apply currying techniques, which will reduce the multiple arguments function by evaluating a sequence of functions with a single argument in each function.

Chapter 3, *Applying Immutable State to the Function*, explains how we implement the immutable object for the mutable object. We will also delve into first-class functions and pure functions, which we discussed in the previous chapter, to produce an immutable object.

Chapter 4, *Repeating Method Invocation Using Recursive Algorithm*, discusses the difference between iteration and recursion and why recursion techniques are better for functional programming. We will also enumerate the three kinds of recursion: functional, procedural, and backtracking recursion.

Chapter 5, *Procrastinating the Execution Process Using Lazy Evaluation*, explains how to delay the process of execution to get more efficient code. We will also implement caching and memoization techniques to make our code run faster.

Chapter 6, *Optimizing Code with Metaprogramming*, talks about running code with compile-time execution by using metaprogramming to optimize code. We will also discuss how to refactor flow control into template metaprogramming.

Chapter 7, *Running Parallel Execution Using Concurrency*, walks us through running multiple threads in C++ programming, as well as synchronizing threads to avoid deadlocks. We will also apply thread processing in a Windows operating system.

Chapter 8, *Creating and Debugging Application in Functional Approach*, elaborates all the techniques we discussed in the previous chapters to design a functional programming. Also, we will try to debug code to find a solution if there are unexpected results or the program crashes in the middle of execution.

What you need for this book

To walk through this book and successfully compile all the source code examples, you will require a personal computer that runs Microsoft Windows 8.1 (or later) and contains the following software:

- The latest version of GCC, which supports C++11, C++14, and C++17 (during the writing of this book, the latest version was GCC v7.1.0)
- The Microsoft C++ compiler provided in Microsoft Visual Studio 2017 for supporting C++11, C++14, and C++17 (for Chapter 7, *Running Parallel Execution Using Concurrency*)
- Code::Blocks v16.01 (all sample code is written using the Code::Blocks IDE; however, it's optional to use this IDE)

Who this book is for

This book is for C++ developers comfortable with OOP who are interested in learning how to apply the functional paradigm to create robust and testable apps.

Conventions

In this book, you will find a number of text styles that distinguish between different kinds of information. Here are some examples of these styles and an explanation of their meaning.

Code words in text, database table names, folder names, filenames, file extensions, pathnames, dummy URLs, and user input are shown as follows: "the `auto` keyword can also be applied to a function to deduce a function's return type automatically."

A block of code is set as follows:

```
int add(int i, int j)
{
  return i + j;
}
```

When we wish to draw your attention to a particular part of a code block, the relevant lines or items are set in bold:

```
// Initializing a string variable
Name n = {"Frankie Kaur"};
cout << "Initial name = " << n.str;
cout << endl;
```

New terms and **important words** are shown in bold.

Warnings or important notes appear like this.

Tips and tricks appear like this.

Reader feedback

Feedback from our readers is always welcome. Let us know what you think about this book—what you liked or disliked. Reader feedback is important for us as it helps us develop titles that you will really get the most out of.

To send us general feedback, simply e-mail feedback@packtpub.com, and mention the book's title in the subject of your message.

If there is a topic that you have expertise in and you are interested in either writing or contributing to a book, see our author guide at www.packtpub.com/authors.

Customer support

Now that you are the proud owner of a Packt book, we have a number of things to help you to get the most from your purchase.

Downloading the example code

You can download the example code files for this book from your account at http://www.packtpub.com. If you purchased this book elsewhere, you can visit http://www.packtpub.com/support and register to have the files e-mailed directly to you.

You can download the code files by following these steps:

1. Log in or register to our website using your e-mail address and password.
2. Hover the mouse pointer on the **SUPPORT** tab at the top.
3. Click on **Code Downloads & Errata**.
4. Enter the name of the book in the **Search** box.
5. Select the book for which you're looking to download the code files.
6. Choose from the drop-down menu where you purchased this book from.
7. Click on **Code Download**.

Once the file is downloaded, please make sure that you unzip or extract the folder using the latest version of:

- WinRAR / 7-Zip for Windows
- Zipeg / iZip / UnRarX for Mac
- 7-Zip / PeaZip for Linux

The code bundle for the book is also hosted on GitHub at `https://github.com/PacktPubl ishing/LearningCPPFunctionalProgramming`. We also have other code bundles from our rich catalog of books and videos available at `https://github.com/PacktPublishing/`. Check them out!

Downloading the color images of this book

We also provide you with a PDF file that has color images of the screenshots/diagrams used in this book. The color images will help you better understand the changes in the output. You can download this file from `https://www.packtpub.com/sites/default/files/down loads/LearningCPPFunctionalProgramming_ColorImages.pdf`.

Errata

Although we have taken every care to ensure the accuracy of our content, mistakes do happen. If you find a mistake in one of our books—maybe a mistake in the text or the code—we would be grateful if you could report this to us. By doing so, you can save other readers from frustration and help us improve subsequent versions of this book. If you find any errata, please report them by visiting `http://www.packtpub.com/submit-errata`, selecting your book, clicking on the **Errata Submission Form** link, and entering the details of your errata. Once your errata are verified, your submission will be accepted and the errata will be uploaded to our website or added to any list of existing errata under the Errata section of that title.

To view the previously submitted errata, go to `https://www.packtpub.com/books/conten t/support` and enter the name of the book in the search field. The required information will appear under the **Errata** section.

Piracy

Piracy of copyrighted material on the Internet is an ongoing problem across all media. At Packt, we take the protection of our copyright and licenses very seriously. If you come across any illegal copies of our works in any form on the Internet, please provide us with the location address or website name immediately so that we can pursue a remedy.

Please contact us at `copyright@packtpub.com` with a link to the suspected pirated material.

We appreciate your help in protecting our authors and our ability to bring you valuable content.

Questions

If you have a problem with any aspect of this book, you can contact us at questions@packtpub.com, and we will do our best to address the problem.

1
Diving into Modern C++

The C++ programming language has been changed dramatically since its invention in 1979. Some people in this era might be a little bit scared to code using C++ language since it is not user-friendly. The memory management we have to deal with sometimes makes people unwilling to use this language. Fortunately, since **C++11**--also known as **modern C++**, along with **C++14** and **C++17**--has been released, numerous features have been introduced to simplify our code in the C++ language. Moreover, the best part of it is that the C++ programming language is a great language for any project, from low-level programming to web programming, as well as functional programming.

This chapter is the best place to start our journey in this book, as it is addressed to the C++ programmers to refresh their knowledge and will discuss the following topics:

- Understanding several new features in modern C++
- Implementing the C++ Standard Libraries in modern C++
- The use of the Lambda expression and all features included in C++ Lambda
- Using smart pointer to avoid manual memory management
- Dealing with many return values using tuples

Getting closer with several new features in modern C++

So, what is new in modern C++ in comparison to the old one? There are so many changes in modern C++ compared to the old one, and the book pages will dramatically increase if we discuss all of them. However, we will discuss the new features in modern C++, which we should know about, to make us more productive in coding activities. We will discuss several new keywords, such as `auto`, `decltype`, and `nullptr`. We will also discuss the enhancement of the `begin()` and `end()` function that has now become a non-member class function. We will also discuss the augmented support for the `for-each` technique to iterate over collections using the `range-based for loop` techniques.

The next few subsections in this chapter will also discuss the new features of modern C++, namely Lambda expressions, smart pointers, and tuples, which were just added in the C++11 release.

Defining the data type automatically using the auto keyword

Prior to the modern C++, the C++ language has a keyword named `auto` that is used to explicitly specify that the variable should have **automatic duration**. The automatic duration that adheres to the variable will create the variable at the point of definition (and initialized, if relevant) and destroy the variable when the block they are defined in is exited. For instance, the local variable will be created when it is defined at the beginning of the function and destroyed when the program exits the function where the local variable is there.

Since C++11, the `auto` keyword is used to tell the compiler to deduce the actual type of a variable that is being declared from its initializer. And since C++14, the keyword can also be applied to a function to specify the return type of the function that is a trailing return type. Now, in modern C++, the use of the `auto` keyword to specify the automatic duration is abolished since all variables are set to automatic duration by default.

The following is an `auto.cpp` code demonstrating the use of the `auto` keyword in the variables. We will define four variables with the `auto` keyword, and then find out the data type for each variable using the `typeid()` function. Let's take a look:

```
/* auto.cpp */

#include <iostream>
#include <typeinfo>
```

```cpp
int main()
{
    std::cout << "[auto.cpp]" << std::endl;

    // Creating several auto-type variables
    auto a = 1;
    auto b = 1.0;
    auto c = a + b;
    auto d = {b, c};

    // Displaying the preceding variables' type
    std::cout << "type of a: " << typeid(a).name() << std::endl;
    std::cout << "type of b: " << typeid(b).name() << std::endl;
    std::cout << "type of c: " << typeid(c).name() << std::endl;
    std::cout << "type of d: " << typeid(d).name() << std::endl;
    return 0;
}
```

As we can see in the preceding code, we have an a variable that will store the integer value and have a b variable that will store the double value. We calculate the addition of a and b and store the result in variable c. Here, we expect that c will store the double object since we add the integer and double object. The last is the d variable that will store the initializer_list<double> data type. When we run the preceding code, we will see the following output on the console:

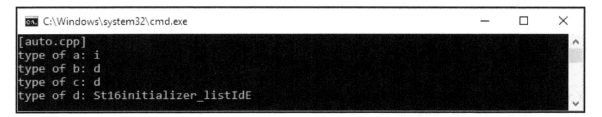

As can be seen in the preceding snapshot, we are just given the first character of the data type, such as i for integer, d for double, and St16initializer_listIdE for initializer_list<double>, that is the last lowercase d character that stands for double.

We may have to enable the **Run-Time Type Information (RTTI)** feature in our compiler options to retrieve the data type object. However, GCC has enabled the feature by default. Also, the output of the use of the typeid() function depends on the compiler. We may get the raw type name or just a symbol as we did in the preceding example.

Besides, for variable, as we discussed earlier, the `auto` keyword can also be applied to a function to deduce a function's return type automatically. Suppose we have the following trivial function named `add()` to calculate the addition of two parameters:

```
int add(int i, int j)
{
    return i + j;
}
```

We can refactor the preceding method to use the `auto` keyword, as we can see in the following lines of code:

```
auto add(int i, int j)
{
    return i + j;
}
```

Similar to the auto-type variable, the compiler can decide the correct return type based on the returned value of the function. And, as shown in the preceding code, the function will indeed return the integer value since we just add two integer values.

Another feature that uses the `auto` keyword in modern C++ is trailing the return type syntax. By using this feature, we can specify the return type, the rest of the function prototype, or function signature. From the preceding code, we can refactor it to use the feature as follows:

```
auto add(int i, int j) -> int
{
    return i + j;
}
```

You might ask me why we have to specify the data type again after the arrow symbol (->), even though we have used the `auto` keyword. We will find the answer when we cover the `decltype` keyword in the next section. Also, by using this feature, we can now refactor the preceding `auto.cpp` code a little bit by modifying the syntax of the `main()` method, instead of the following syntax of `main()` function signature:

```
int main()
{
    // The body of the function
}
```

We can change the signature syntax into the following line of code:

```
auto main -> int
{
  // The body of the function
}
```

Now, we will see all of our code in this book using this trailing return type feature to apply the modern C++ syntax.

Querying the type of an expression using the decltype keyword

We discussed in the preceding section that the `auto` keyword can automatically deduce the type of the variable based on the type of values it stores. The keyword can also deduce the function's return type based on the type of its return value. Now, let's combine the `auto` keyword and the `decltype` keyword to gain the power of modern C++.

Before we combine the two keywords, we will find out what the `decltype` keyword is used for--it is used for asking the type of an object or an expression. Let's take a look at the following several lines of trivial variable declaration:

```
const int func1();
const int& func2();
int i;

struct X { double d; };
const X* x = new X();
```

Now, based on the preceding code, we can declare other variables using the `decltype` keyword as follows:

```
// Declaring const int variable
// using func1() type
decltype(func1()) f1;

// Declaring const int& variable
// using func2() type
decltype(func2()) f2;

// Declaring int variable
// using i type
decltype(i) i1;
```

```
// Declaring double variable
// using struct X type
decltype(x->d) d1; // type is double
decltype((x->d)) d2; // type is const double&
```

As we can see in the preceding code, we can specify the type of an object based on another object's type. Now, let's suppose we need to refactor the preceding `add()` method to become a template. Without the `auto` and `decltype` keyword, we will have the following template implementation:

```
template<typename I, typename J, typename K>
K add(I i, J j)
{
  return i + j;
}
```

Fortunately, since the `auto` keyword can specify the return type of the function, which is a trailing return type, and the `decltype` keyword can deduce the type based on the expression, we can refactor the preceding template as follows:

```
template<typename I, typename J>
auto add(I i, J j) -> decltype(i + j)
{
  return i + j;
}
```

To prove, let's compile and run the following `decltype.cpp` code. We will use the following template to calculate the addition of two different value types--`integer` and `double`:

```
/* decltype.cpp */
#include <iostream>

// Creating template
template<typename I, typename J>
auto add(I i, J j) -> decltype(i + j)
{
  return i + j;
}

auto main() -> int
{
  std::cout << "[decltype.cpp]" << std::endl;

  // Consuming the template
  auto d = add<int, double>(2, 2.5);
```

```
    // Displaying the preceding variables' type
    std::cout << "result of 2 + 2.5: " << d << std::endl;

    return 0;
}
```

The compilation process should run smoothly without error. We will see the following output on the screen if we run the preceding code:

As we can see, we have successfully combined the auto and decltype keyword to create a template simpler than we usually do before the modern C++ is announced.

Pointing to a null pointer

Another new feature in modern C++ is a keyword named nullptr that replaces the NULL macro to represent a null pointer. Now, there's no ambiguity in the use of the NULL macro for zero numeric or a null pointer. Let's suppose we have the following two method's signature in our declaration:

```
void funct(const char *);
void funct(int)
```

The former function will pass a pointer as the argument and the latter will pass the integer number as its argument. Then, we invoke the funct() method and pass the NULL macro as the parameter, as shown here:

```
funct(NULL);
```

What we intend to call is the former function. However, since we pass the NULL parameters, which is basically defined as 0, the latter function will be invoked. In modern C++, we can use the nullptr keyword to ensure that we will pass a null pointer to the argument. The invocation of the funct() method should be as follows:

```
funct(nullptr);
```

Now the compiler will invoke the former function since it passes a null pointer to the argument, and this is what we expect. There will be no ambiguity anymore, and it will avoid unnecessary future problems.

Returning an iterator using non-member begin() and end() function

Prior to modern C++, to iterate a sequence, we call the `begin()` and `end()` member method of each container. For array, we can iterate its element by iterating the index. Since C++11, the language has a non-member function--`begin()` and `end()`--to retrieve the iterator of the sequence. Let's suppose we have an array of the following elements:

```
int arr[] = { 0, 1, 2, 3, 4, 5, 6, 7, 8, 9 };
```

When the language doesn't have the `begin()` and `end()` function, we need to iterate the elements of the array using the index we can see in the following lines of code:

```
for (unsigned int i = 0; i < sizeof(arr)/sizeof(arr[0]); ++i)
// Do something to the array
```

Fortunately, using the `begin()` and `end()` function, we can refactor the preceding `for` loop to become as follows:

```
for (auto i = std::begin(arr); i != std::end(arr); ++i)
// Do something to the array
```

As we can see, the use of the `begin()` and `end()` function creates a compact code since we don't need to worry about the length of the array because the iterator pointer of `begin()` and `end()` will do it for us. For comparison, let's take a look at the following `begin_end.cpp` code:

```cpp
/* begin_end.cpp */
#include <iostream>

auto main() -> int
{
  std::cout << "[begin_end.cpp]" << std::endl;

  // Declaring an array
  int arr[] = { 0, 1, 2, 3, 4, 5, 6, 7, 8, 9 };

  // Displaying the array elements
  // using conventional for-loop
  std::cout << "Displaying array element using conventional for-
    loop";
  std::cout << std::endl;
  for (unsigned int i = 0; i < sizeof(arr)/sizeof(arr[0]); ++i)
  std::cout << arr[i] << " ";
  std::cout << std::endl;
```

```
// Displaying the array elements
// using non-member begin() and end()
std::cout << "Displaying array element using non-member begin()
 and end()";
std::cout << std::endl;
for (auto i = std::begin(arr); i != std::end(arr); ++i)
 std::cout << *i << " ";
std::cout << std::endl;

return 0;
}
```

To prove the preceding code, we can compile the code, and, when we run it, the following output should be displayed on the console screen:

```
Command Prompt                                          —    □    ✕
[begin_end.cpp]
Displaying array element using conventional for-loop
0 1 2 3 4 5 6 7 8 9
Displaying array element using non-member begin() and end()
0 1 2 3 4 5 6 7 8 9
```

As we can see in the screenshot, we've got the exact same output when we use the conventional `for-loop` or `begin()` and `end()` functions.

Iterating over collections using range-based for loops

In the modern C++, there is a new feature that is augmented to support the `for-each` technique to iterate over collections. This feature is useful if you want to do something to the elements of a collection or array without caring about the number of elements or the indexes. The syntax of the feature is also simple. Suppose we have an array named `arr` and we want to iterate each element using the `range-based for loop` technique; we can use the following syntax:

```
for (auto a : arr)
// Do something with a
```

So, we can refactor our preceding `begin_end.cpp` code to use `range-based for loop` as we can see in the following code:

```
/* range_based_for_loop.cpp */
#include <iostream>

auto main() -> int
{
  std::cout << "[range_based_for_loop.cpp]" << std::endl;

  // Declaring an array
  int arr[] = {0, 1, 2, 3, 4, 5, 6, 7, 8, 9};

  // Displaying the array elements
  // using non-member begin() and end()
  std::cout << "Displaying array element using range-based for
    loop";
  std::cout << std::endl;
  for (auto a : arr) std::cout << a << " ";
  std::cout << std::endl;

  return 0;
}
```

The syntax we see in the preceding code is simpler now. If we compile the preceding code, we should find no error and, if we run the code, we should see the following output on the console screen:

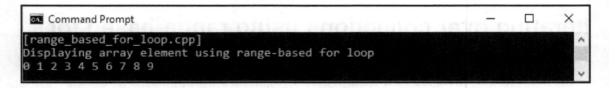

We now have a new technique to iterate over the collection without caring about the indexes of the collection. We will keep using it in this book.

Leveraging the use of C++ language with the C++ Standard Libraries

The C++ Standard Libraries are a powerful set of classes and functions that have many capabilities needed to create an application. They are controlled by the C++ ISO Standard Committee and is influenced by the **Standard Template Libraries** (STL), which were the generic libraries before C++11 was introduced. All features in Standard Libraries are declared in `std namespace` and no headers end in `.h` anymore (except 18 headers of the ISO C90 C Standard Library that is incorporated into the C++ Standard Libraries).

There are several header files containing the declaration of the C++ Standard Libraries. However, it is almost impossible to discuss all header files in these tiny chapters. We will, therefore, talk about some features that we will use most in our daily coding activities.

Placing any objects in the container

Container is an object that is used to store other objects and manage the memory that is used by the objects it contains. An array is a new feature added in C++11 to store the collection of specific data types. It is a sequence container since it stores the same data type objects and arranges them linearly. Let's take a look at the following code snippet:

```cpp
/* array.cpp */
#include <array>
#include <iostream>

auto main() -> int
{
  std::cout << "[array.cpp]" << std::endl;

  // Initializing an array containing five integer elements
  std::array<int, 10> arr = { 0, 1, 2, 3, 4, 5, 6, 7, 8, 9 };

  // Displaying the original elements of the array
  std::cout << "Original Data : ";
  for(auto a : arr) std::cout << a << " ";
  std::cout << std::endl;

  // Modifying the content of
  // the 1st and 3rd element of the array
  arr[1] = 9;
  arr[3] = 7;

  // Displaying the altered array elements
```

```
      std::cout << "Manipulated Data: ";
      for(auto a : arr) std::cout << a << " ";
      std::cout << std::endl;

      return 0;
}
```

As we can see in the preceding code, we instance a new array named `arr`, set its length as `10`, and only approve the `int` element. As we can guess, the output of the code is a line of numbers `0` through `9`, which is shown in the original data, and the other line will show the altered data, as we can see in the following screenshot:

```
[array.cpp]
Original Data   : 0 1 2 3 4 5 6 7 8 9
Manipulated Data: 0 9 2 7 4 5 6 7 8 9
```

There is no performance issue if we declare an array using `std::array`; we use in the `array.cpp` code and compare it with a usual array as we use in the `begin_end.cpp` code. However, in modern C++, we are given a new array declaration that has a friendly value semantic, so that it can be passed to or returned from functions by value. Also, the interface of this new array declaration makes it more convenient to find the size, and use it with **Standard Template Library** (**STL**)-style iterator-based algorithms.

It is good to use an array as the container since we can store the data and manipulate them. We can also sort and find a specific element if we want. However, since the array is a compile-time non-resizable object, we have to decide the size of the array we intend to use at the very beginning as we cannot change the size later. In other words, we cannot insert or remove the element from the existing array. As a solution to this problem, and for the best practice of using the container as well, we can now use a `vector` to store our collection. Let's take a look at the following code:

```
/* vector.cpp */
#include <vector>
#include <iostream>

auto main() -> int
{
  std::cout << "[vector.cpp]" << std::endl;

  // Initializing a vector containing three integer elements
  std::vector<int> vect = { 0, 1, 2 };
```

```
    // Displaying the original elements of the vector
    std::cout << "Original Data : ";
    for (auto v : vect) std::cout << v << " ";
    std::cout << std::endl;

    // Adding two new data
    vect.push_back(3);
    vect.push_back(4);

    // Displaying the elements of the new vector
    // and reverse the order
    std::cout << "New Data Added : ";
    for (auto v : vect) std::cout << v << " ";
    std::cout << std::endl;

    // Modifying the content of
    // the 2nd and 4th element of the vector
    vect.at(2) = 5;
    vect.at(4) = 6;

    // Displaying the altered array elements
    std::cout << "Manipulate Data: ";
    for (auto v : vect) std::cout << v << " ";
    std::cout << std::endl;

    return 0;
}
```

Now, we have a `vector` instance in our preceding code instead of an `array` instance. As we can see, we give an additional value for the `vector` instance using the `push_back()` method. We can add the value anytime we want. The manipulation of each element is also easier since `vector` has an `at()` method that returns a reference to the element of the specific index. The following screenshot is what we will see as the output when running the code:

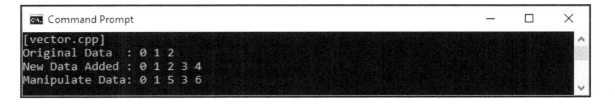

It is better to always use the `at()` method instead of the `[]` operator when we want to access the specific element by its index in a `vector` instance. It's because, when we accidentally access the out of range position, the `at()` method will throw an `out_of_range` exception. Otherwise, the `[]` operator will give undefined behavior.

Using algorithms

We can sort the elements of the collection we have in `array` or `vector`, as well as find specific content of the element. For these purposes, we have to use the algorithm feature provided by the C++ Standard Library. Let's take a look at the following code to demonstrate the sorting element capability in the algorithm feature:

```cpp
/* sort.cpp */
#include <vector>
#include <algorithm>
#include <iostream>

bool comparer(int a, int b)
{
  return (a > b);
}

auto main() -> int
{
  std::cout << "[sort.cpp]" << std::endl;

  // Initializing a vector containing several integer elements
  std::vector<int> vect = { 20, 43, 11, 78, 5, 96 };

  // Displaying the original elements of the vector
  std::cout << "Original Data : ";
  for (auto v : vect)
  std::cout << v << " ";
  std::cout << std::endl;

  // Sorting the vector element ascending
  std::sort(std::begin(vect), std::end(vect));

  // Displaying the ascending sorted elements
  // of the vector
  std::cout << "Ascending Sorted : ";
  for (auto v : vect)
  std::cout << v << " ";
  std::cout << std::endl;
```

```
    // Sorting the vector element descending
    // using comparer
    std::sort(std::begin(vect), std::end(vect), comparer);

    // Displaying the descending sorted elements
    // of the vector
    std::cout << "Descending Sorted: ";
    for (auto v : vect)
    std::cout << v << " ";
    std::cout << std::endl;

    return 0;
}
```

As we see in the preceding code, we invoked the sort() method twice. First, we just supplied the range of the elements we wanted to sort. Then we added the comparison function, comparer(), to be provided to the sort() method to gain more flexibility the method has. The output we will see on the console from the preceding code is as follows:

```
Command Prompt                                        —    □    ×
[sort.cpp]
Original Data    : 20 43 11 78 5 96
Ascending Sorted : 5 11 20 43 78 96
Descending Sorted: 96 78 43 20 11 5
```

From the preceding screenshot, we can see that we have six elements in a vector at the beginning. We then sort the elements of the vector using a simple sort() method. Then, we invoke the sort() method again, but instead of a simple sort() method, we now supply comparer() to the sort() method. As a result, the vector elements will be sorted descendingly since the comparer() function looks for the greater value from two inputs.

Now, let's move to another capability the algorithm feature has, which is finding a particular element. Let's suppose we have the Vehicle class in our code. It has two private fields named m_vehicleType and m_totalOfWheel, and we can retrieve the value from the getter methods named GetType() and GetNumOfWheel() respectively. It also has two constructors, which are the default constructor and the user-defined one. The declaration of the class should be as follows:

```
/* vehicle.h */
#ifndef __VEHICLE_H__
#define __VEHICLE_H__
```

```
#include <string>

class Vehicle
{
  private:
    std::string vehicleType;
    int totalOfWheel;

  public:
    Vehicle(
      const std::string &type,
      int _wheel);
    Vehicle();
    ~Vehicle();
    std::string GetType() const {return vehicleType;}
    int GetNumOfWheel() const {return totalOfWheel;}
};

#endif // End of __VEHICLE_H__
```

The implementation of the Vehicle class is as follows:

```
/* vehicle.cpp */
#include "vehicle.h"

using namespace std;

// Constructor with default value for
// m_vehicleType and m_totalOfWheel
Vehicle::Vehicle() : m_totalOfWheel(0)
{
}

// Constructor with user-defined value for
// m_vehicleType and m_totalOfWheel
Vehicle::Vehicle( const string &type, int wheel) :
 m_vehicleType(type),
 m_totalOfWheel(wheel)
{
}

// Destructor
Vehicle::~Vehicle()
{
}
```

We will store a collection of `Vehicle` in the `vector` container, and then we will search for some elements based on its property. The code will be as follows:

```cpp
/* find.cpp */
#include <vector>
#include <algorithm>
#include <iostream>
#include "../vehicle/vehicle.h"

using namespace std;
bool TwoWheeled(const Vehicle &vehicle)
{
  return _vehicle.GetNumOfWheel() == 2 ?
    true : false;
 }

auto main() -> int
{
  cout << "[find.cpp]" << endl;

  // Initializing several Vehicle instances
  Vehicle car("car", 4);
  Vehicle motorcycle("motorcycle", 2);
  Vehicle bicycle("bicycle", 2);
  Vehicle bus("bus", 6);
  // Assigning the preceding Vehicle instances to a vector
  vector<Vehicle> vehicles = { car, motorcycle, bicycle, bus };

  // Displaying the elements of the vector
  cout << "All vehicles:" << endl;;
  for (auto v : vehicles)
    std::cout << v.GetType() << endl;
  cout << endl;

  // Displaying the elements of the vector
  // which are the two-wheeled vehicles
  cout << "Two-wheeled vehicle(s):" << endl;;
  auto tw = find_if(
                begin(vehicles),
                end(vehicles),
                TwoWheeled);
  while (tw != end(vehicles))
  {
    cout << tw->GetType() << endl ;
    tw = find_if(++tw, end(vehicles), TwoWheeled);
  }
  cout << endl;
```

```
        // Displaying the elements of the vector
        // which are not the two-wheeled vehicles
        cout << "Not the two-wheeled vehicle(s):" << endl;;
        auto ntw = find_if_not(begin(vehicles),
                               end(vehicles),
                               TwoWheeled);
        while (ntw != end(vehicles))
        {
            cout << ntw->GetType() << endl ;
            ntw = find_if_not(++ntw, end(vehicles), TwoWheeled);
        }

        return 0;
    }
```

As we can see, we instance four Vehicle objects, then store them in vector. There, we try to find the vehicle that has two wheels. The find_if() function is used for this purpose. We also have the TwoWheeled() method to provide the comparison value. Since we are finding the two-wheeled vehicle, we will inspect the totalOfWheel variable in the Vehicle class by invoking the GetNumOfWheel() method. In contrast, if we want to find the element that doesn't conform to the comparison value, we can use the find_if_not() function, which had been added in C++11. The output we get should look like this:

```
Command Prompt                                         —    □    ×
[find.cpp]
All vehicles:
car
motorcycle
bicycle
bus

Two-wheeled vehicle(s):
motorcycle
bicycle

Not the two-wheeled vehicle(s):
car
bus
```

As we can see in the `vehicle.cpp` code and `find.cpp` code, we now add the `using namespace std;` line in the `*.cpp` files. We do this to make our coding activity become more productive since we don't have to type many words. In contrast, in `vehicle.h`, we still using `std::` followed by the methods or properties name rather than use the std namespace at the beginning. It's best practice to not declare `using namespace` in header files since the header files are the files we will deliver if we create some libraries for instances. The user of our library may have another method with the same name as the function our library has. It will definitely create conflict between these two functions.

Another algorithm feature we will use most is the `for_each` loop. Instead of using the `for` loop, the use of the `for_each` loop will make our code more concise in many cases. It's also simpler and less error prone than a `for` loop because we can define a specific function for the `for_each` loop. Now let's refactor our previous code to use the `for_each` loop. The code is written as follows:

```cpp
/* for_each.cpp */
#include <vector>
#include <algorithm>
#include <iostream>
#include "vehicle.h"

using namespace std;

void PrintOut(const Vehicle &vehicle)
{
    cout << vehicle.GetType() << endl;
}

auto main() -> int
{
    cout << "[for_each.cpp]" << endl;

    // Initializing several Vehicle instances
    Vehicle car("car", 4);
    Vehicle motorcycle("motorcycle", 2);
    Vehicle bicycle("bicycle", 2);
    Vehicle bus("bus", 6);

    // Assigning the preceding Vehicle instances to a vector
    vector<Vehicle> vehicles = { car, motorcycle, bicycle, bus };

    // Displaying the elements of the vector
    cout << "All vehicles:" << endl;
```

```
    for_each(begin(vehicles), end(vehicles), PrintOut);

    return 0;
}
```

Now, with the `for_each` loop, we have a clearer code. We only need to provide the first and last iterator and then pass a function--the `PrintOut()` function in this case--that will be invoked in each element in the range.

Simplifying the function notation using a Lambda expression

The Lambda expression is an anonymous notation that represents something that performs an operation or calculation. In functional programming, the Lambda expression is useful to produce the first class and pure function, which we will discuss in separate chapters in this book. For now, let's familiarize ourselves with this new feature introduced in C++11 by investigating three basic parts of the Lambda expression:

- capturing list: []
- parameter list: ()
- body: {}

The order of these three basic parts is as follows:

```
[] () {}
```

The capturing list part is also used as a mark to identify the Lambda expression. It is a placeholder to value to be involved in the expression. The only capture defaults are the ampersand symbol (&), which will implicitly capture the automatic variables by reference, and the equal sign (=), which will implicitly capture the automatic variables by copy (we will discuss it further in the upcoming section). The parameter list is similar to the capturing list in every function where we can pass the value to it. The body is the implementation of the function itself.

Using the Lambda expression for a tiny function

Imagine we have a tiny one-line function that we invoke only once. It's better if we write the operation of that function directly when we need it. We actually had this function in our previous example when discussing the C++ Standard Library. Just go back to the `for_each.cpp` file and we will find the `PrintOut()` function that is only invoked once by `for_each()`. We can make this `for_each` loop more readable if we use Lambda. Let's take a look at the following code snippet to examine how we refactor the `for_each.cpp` file:

```cpp
/* lambda_tiny_func.cpp */
#include <vector>
#include <algorithm>
#include <iostream>
#include "../vehicle/vehicle.h"

using namespace std;

auto main() -> int
{
  cout << "[lambda_tiny_func.cpp]" << endl;

  // Initializing several Vehicle instances
  Vehicle car("car", 4);
  Vehicle motorcycle("motorcycle", 2);
  Vehicle bicycle("bicycle", 2);
  Vehicle bus("bus", 6);

  // Assigning the preceding Vehicle instances to a vector
  vector<Vehicle> vehicles = { car, motorcycle, bicycle, bus };

  // Displaying the elements of the vector
  // using Lambda expression
  cout << "All vehicles:" << endl;
  for_each(
        begin(vehicles),
        end(vehicles),
        [](const Vehicle &vehicle){
            cout << vehicle.GetType() << endl;
        });

  return 0;
}
```

As we can see, we have transformed the `PrintOut()` function that we used in the `for_each.cpp` file into a Lambda expression and passed it to the `for_each` loop. It will indeed give the same output as the `for_each.cpp` file does. However, now our code becomes more concise and readable.

Using the Lambda expression for multiline functions

The Lambda expression can also be used for multiline functions, so we can put the body of the function on it. This will make our code more readable as well. Let's make a new code. In that code, we will have an integer collection and an intent to inspect whether the selected element is the prime number or not. We can make a separate function, for instance, `PrintPrime()`, then invoke it. However, since the prime number checking operation is called only once, it's more readable if we transform it into a Lambda expression. The code should look like this:

```cpp
/* lambda_multiline_func.cpp */
#include <vector>
#include <algorithm>
#include <iostream>

using namespace std;

auto main() -> int
{
  cout << "[lambda_multiline_func.cpp]" << endl;

  // Initializing a vector containing integer element
  vector<int> vect;
  for (int i = 0; i < 10; ++i)
    vect.push_back(i);

  // Displaying whether or not the element is prime number
  for_each(
        begin(vect),
        end(vect),
        [](int n) {
          cout << n << " is";
          if(n < 2)
          {
            if(n == 0)
            cout << " not";
          }
          else
```

```
        {
          for (int j = 2; j < n; ++j)
            {
                if (n % j == 0)
                {
                  cout << " not";
                  break;
                }
            }
        }

        cout << " prime number" << endl;
    });

    return 0;
}
```

The output we should see on the screen is as follows:

```
Command Prompt                                          —    □    ×
[lambda_multiline_func.cpp]
0 is not prime number
1 is prime number
2 is prime number
3 is prime number
4 is not prime number
5 is prime number
6 is not prime number
7 is prime number
8 is not prime number
9 is not prime number
```

As we can see in the preceding screenshot, we have successfully identified the prime number by using the Lambda expression.

Returning a value from the Lambda expression

Our two preceding samples of the Lambda expression are just for the purpose to print on console. It means the function does not need to return any value. However, we can ask the Lambda expression to return a value for an instance if we do the calculation inside the function and return the calculation result. Let's take a look at the following code to examine the use of this Lambda:

```cpp
/* lambda_returning_value.cpp */
#include <vector>
#include <algorithm>
#include <iostream>

using namespace std;

auto main() -> int
{
  cout << "[lambda_returning_value.cpp]" << endl;

  // Initializing a vector containing integer element
  vector<int> vect;
  for (int i = 0; i < 10; ++i)
    vect.push_back(i);

  // Displaying the elements of vect
  cout << "Original Data:" << endl;
  for_each(
        begin(vect),
        end(vect),
        [](int n){
            cout << n << " ";
        });
  cout << endl;

  // Creating another vect2 vector
  vector<int> vect2;
  // Resize the size of vect2 exactly same with vect
  vect2.resize(vect.size());
  // Doubling the elements of vect and store to vect2
  transform(
        begin(vect),
        end(vect),
        begin(vect2),
        [](int n) {
            return n * n;
        });
```

```
// Displaying the elements of vect2
cout << "Squared Data:" << endl;
for_each(
        begin(vect2),
        end(vect2),
        [](int n) {
            cout << n << " ";
        });
cout << endl;

// Creating another vect3 vector
vector<double> vect3;
// Resize the size of vect3 exactly same with vect
vect3.resize(vect.size());
// Finding the average of the elements of vect
// and store to vect2
transform(
        begin(vect2),
        end(vect2),
        begin(vect3),
        [](int n) -> double {
            return n / 2.0;
        });

// Displaying the elements of vect3
cout << "Average Data:" << endl;
for_each(
        begin(vect3),
        end(vect3),
        [](double d) {
            cout << d << " ";
        });
cout << endl;

return 0;
}
```

When we use the `transform()` method in the preceding code, we have a Lambda expression that returns a value from the calculation of n * n. However, there's no return type stated in the expression. This is because we can omit the statement of the return type since the compiler has understood that the expression will return an `integer` value. So, after we have another vector, `vect2`, which has the same size as `vect`, we can invoke the `transform()` method along with the Lambda expression, and the value of `vect` will be doubled and stored in `vect2`.

We can, if we want to, specify the return type to the Lambda expression. As we can see in the preceding code, we transformed the vect3 vector based on all values of the vect vector, but now we specify the return type to double using the arrow symbol (–>). The result of the preceding code should be like the following screenshot:

```
[lambda_returning_value.cpp]
Original Data:
0 1 2 3 4 5 6 7 8 9
Squared Data:
0 1 4 9 16 25 36 49 64 81
Average Data:
0 0.5 2 4.5 8 12.5 18 24.5 32 40.5
```

As we can see from the preceding screenshot, we have successfully found the doubled and average result using the Lambda expression.

Capturing a value to the Lambda expression

In our previous Lambda expression examples, we keep the capturing part and the square bracket ([]) empty since the Lambda doesn't capture anything and doesn't have any extra member variable in the anonymous object generated by the compiler. We can also specify the object we want to capture in the Lambda expression by specifying it in this square bracket. Let's take a look at the following piece of code to go through the discussion:

```cpp
/* lambda_capturing_by_value.cpp */
#include <vector>
#include <algorithm>
#include <iostream>

using namespace std;

auto main() -> int
{
  cout << "[lambda_capturing_by_value.cpp]" << endl;

  // Initializing a vector containing integer element
  vector<int> vect;
  for (int i = 0; i < 10; ++i)
  vect.push_back(i);

  // Displaying the elements of vect
```

```
cout << "Original Data:" << endl;
for_each(
        begin(vect),
        end(vect),
        [](int n){
            cout << n << " ";
        });
cout << endl;

// Initializing two variables
int a = 2;
int b = 8;

// Capturing value explicitly from the two variables
cout << "Printing elements between " << a;
cout << " and " << b << " explicitly [a,b]:" << endl;
for_each(
        begin(vect),
        end(vect),
        [a,b](int n){
            if (n >= a && n <= b)
            cout << n << " ";
        });
cout << endl;

// Modifying variable a and b
a = 3;
b = 7;

// Capturing value implicitly from the two variables
cout << "printing elements between " << a;
cout << " and " << b << " implicitly[=]:" << endl;
for_each(
        begin(vect),
        end(vect),
        [=](int n){
            if (n >= a && n <= b)
            cout << n << " ";
        });
cout << endl;

return 0;
}
```

In the preceding code, we will try to capture the value in the Lambda expression, explicitly and implicitly. Let's suppose we have two variables, a and b, and we want to explicitly capture the values, we can specify them in the Lambda expression using the [a,b] statement, and then using the values inside the function body. Moreover, if we wish to capture the value implicitly, just use [=] for the capturing part and then the expression will know which variable we intend to use when we specify them in the function body. If we run the preceding code, we will get the following output on the screen:

```
Command Prompt                                    —    □    ×
[lambda_capturing_by_value.cpp]
Original Data:
0 1 2 3 4 5 6 7 8 9
Printing elements between 2 and 8 explicitly [a,b]:
2 3 4 5 6 7 8
printing elements between 3 and 7 implicitly[=]:
3 4 5 6 7
```

We can also mutate the state of the values we capture without modifying the value outside the Lambda expression function body. For this purpose, we can use the same techniques as used previously, and add the mutable keyword as shown in the following block of code:

```cpp
/* lambda_capturing_by_value_mutable.cpp */
#include <vector>
#include <algorithm>
#include <iostream>

using namespace std;

auto main() -> int
{
  cout << "[lambda_capturing_by_value_mutable.cpp]" << endl;

  // Initializing a vector containing integer element
  vector<int> vect;
  for (int i = 0; i < 10; ++i)
    vect.push_back(i);

  // Displaying the elements of vect
  cout << "Original Data:" << endl;
  for_each(
          begin(vect),
          end(vect),
          [](int n){
              cout << n << " ";
```

```
            });
    cout << endl;

    // Initializing two variables
    int a = 1;
    int b = 1;

    // Capturing value from the two variables
    // without mutate them
    for_each(
            begin(vect),
            end(vect),
            [=](int& x) mutable {
                const int old = x;
                x *= 2;
                a = b;
                b = old;
            });

    // Displaying the elements of vect
    cout << "Squared Data:" << endl;
    for_each(
            begin(vect),
            end(vect),
            [](int n) {
                cout << n << " ";
            });
    cout << endl << endl;

    // Displaying value of variable a and b
    cout << "a = " << a << endl;
    cout << "b = " << b << endl;

    return 0;
}
```

The preceding code will double the element of the `vect` vector. It uses capturing by value in the Lambda expression and also the `mutable` keyword. As we can see, we passed the vector element by reference (`int& x`) and multiplied it by two, then changed the value of a and b. However, since we use the `mutable` keyword, the final result of a and b will remain the same, although, we have passed the vector by reference. The output on the console looks like the following screenshot:

```
[lambda_capturing_by_value_mutable.cpp]
Original Data:
0 1 2 3 4 5 6 7 8 9
Squared Data:
0 2 4 6 8 10 12 14 16 18

a = 1
b = 1
```

If we want to change the value of the a and b variables, we have to use the Lambda expression to capture by reference. We can do this by passing the reference to the angle bracket in the Lambda expression, for instance, `[&a, &b]`. For more detail, let's take a look at the following piece of code:

```cpp
/* lambda_capturing_by_reference.cpp */
#include <vector>
#include <algorithm>
#include <iostream>

using namespace std;

auto main() -> int
{
  cout << "[lambda_capturing_by_reference.cpp]" << endl;

  // Initializing a vector containing integer element
  vector<int> vect;
  for (int i = 0; i < 10; ++i)
    vect.push_back(i);

  // Displaying the elements of vect
  cout << "Original Data:" << endl;
  for_each(
        begin(vect),
        end(vect),
        [](int n){
```

```cpp
            cout << n << " ";
        });
    cout << endl;

    // Initializing two variables
    int a = 1;
    int b = 1;

    // Capturing value from the two variables
    // and mutate them
    for_each(
        begin(vect),
        end(vect),
        [&a, &b](int& x){
            const int old = x;
            x *= 2;
            a = b;
            b = old;
        });

    // Displaying the elements of vect
    cout << "Squared Data:" << endl;
    for_each(
        begin(vect),
        end(vect),
        [](int n) {
            cout << n << " ";
        });
    cout << endl << endl;

    // Displaying value of variable a and b
    cout << "a = " << a << endl;
    cout << "b = " << b << endl;

    return 0;
}
```

The preceding code has the same behavior with the
`lambda_capturing_by_value_mutable.cpp` file that will double the element of the
`vect` vector. However, by capturing by reference, it now also modifies the value of `a` and `b`
when they are processed in the `for_each` loop. The `a` and `b` values will be changed at the
end of the code, as we can see in the following screenshot:

```
Command Prompt                                          —    □    ×
[lambda_capturing_by_reference.cpp]
Original Data:
0 1 2 3 4 5 6 7 8 9
Squared Data:
0 2 4 6 8 10 12 14 16 18

a = 8
b = 9
```

Preparing the value using initialization captures

Another great feature of the Lambda expression coming up in C++14 is its initialization
captures. The expression can capture a value of the variable and assign it to the expression's
variable. Let's take a look at the following piece of code implementing the initialization
captures:

```cpp
/* lambda_initialization_captures.cpp */
#include <iostream>

using namespace std;

auto main() -> int
{
  cout << "[lambda_initialization_captures.cpp]" << endl;

  // Initializing a variable
  int a = 5;
  cout << "Initial a = " << a << endl;

  // Initializing value to lambda using the variable
  auto myLambda = [&x = a]() { x += 2; };

  // Executing the Lambda
  myLambda();

  // Displaying a new value of the variable
```

```
    cout << "New a = " << a << endl;

    return 0;
}
```

As we can see in the preceding code, we have an int variable named a with the value 5. The Lambda expression, myLambda, then captures the a value and executes it in the code. The result is that now the a value will be 7 since it is added by 2. The following output screenshot should appear in our console window when we run the preceding code:

```
Command Prompt                                    —    □    ×
[lambda_initialization_captures.cpp]
Initial a = 5
New a    = 7
```

From the preceding snapshot, we see that we can prepare the value to be included in the calculation inside the Lambda expression.

Writing a generic Lambda expression to be used many times with many different data types

Before C++14, we have to specifically state the type of the parameter list. Fortunately, now in C++14, Lambda expressions accept auto as a valid parameter type. Therefore, we can now build a generic Lambda expression as demonstrated in the following code. In that code, we have only one Lambda expression to find out which is the greatest value between two numbers passed to the expression. We will use the auto keyword in parameter declaration so it can be passed by any data type. Therefore, the findMax() function parameters can be passed by both the int and float data type. The code should be as follows:

```
/* lambda_expression_generic.cpp */
#include <iostream>

using namespace std;

auto main() -> int
{
    cout << "[lambda_expression_generic.cpp]" << endl;

    // Creating a generic lambda expression
```

```
auto findMax = [] (auto &x, auto &y){
  return x > y ? x : y; };

// Initializing various variables
int i1 = 5, i2 = 3;
float f1 = 2.5f, f2 = 2.05f;

// Consuming generic lambda expression
// using integer data type
cout << "i1 = 5, i2 = 3" << endl;
cout << "Max: " << findMax(i1, i2) << endl << endl;

// Consuming generic lambda expression
// using double data type
cout << "f1 = 2.5f, f2 = 2.05f" << endl;
cout << "Max: " << findMax(f1, f2) << endl << endl;

return 0;
}
```

The output we will see on the console should be as follows:

```
[lambda_expression_generic.cpp]
i1 = 5, i2 = 3
Max: 5

f1 = 2.5f, f2 = 2.05f
Max: 2.5
```

The C++17 language plans to introduce two new features for the Lambda expression--they are capturing *this, which allows the expression to capture the enclosing object by copy, and the constexpr Lambda expressions, which allows us to use the result of the Lambda expressions and generate constexpr objects at compile time. However, since C++17 has not been released yet, we cannot try it for now.

Avoiding manual memory management with smart pointers

The smart pointers are highly useful and have an essential knowledge in using C++ efficiently. C++11 added many new abilities for the smart pointer we can find in the `memory` header file. For a long time, before C++11, we used `auto_ptr` as a smart pointer. However, it was quite unsafe since it had incompatible copy semantics. It's also deprecated now, and we should not use it anymore. Fortunately, C++ has presented `unique_ptr`, which has a similar functionality, but with additional features, such as adding `deleters` and support for arrays. Anything we can do with `auto_pt`, we can and should do with `unique_ptr` instead. We will discuss `unique_ptr` in depth along with other new smart pointers in C++11--`shared_ptr` and `weak_ptr`.

Replacing a raw pointer using unique_ptr

The next pointer we will see is the `unique_ptr` pointer. It is fast, efficient, and a near drop-in replacement for raw or naked pointers. It provides exclusive ownership semantics, which exclusively owns the object that it points to. By its exclusiveness, it can destroy the object when its destructor is called if it has a non-null pointer. It also cannot be copied due to its exclusiveness. It has no copy constructor and copy assignment. Although it cannot be copied, it can be moved since it provides a move constructor and a move assignment.

These are the methods we can use to construct `unique_ptr`:

```
auto up1 = unique_ptr<int>{};
auto up2 = unique_ptr<int>{ nullptr };
auto up3 = unique_ptr<int>{ new int { 1234 } };
```

Based on the preceding code, `up1` and `up2` will construct two new `unique_ptr` that point to nothing (null), whereas `up3` will point to the address that holds the `1234` value. However, C++14 adds a new library function to construct `unique_ptr`, that is, `make_unique`. So, we can construct a new `unique_ptr` pointer as follows:

```
auto up4 = make_unique<int>(1234);
```

The `up4` variable will also point to the address that holds the `1234` value.

Now, let's take a look at the following block of code:

```cpp
/* unique_ptr_1.cpp */
#include <memory>
#include <iostream>

using namespace std;

struct BodyMass
{
  int Id;
  float Weight;

  BodyMass(int id, float weight) :
    Id(id),
    Weight(weight)
    {
      cout << "BodyMass is constructed!" << endl;
      cout << "Id = " << Id << endl;
      cout << "Weight = " << Weight << endl;
    }
  ~BodyMass()
  {
    cout << "BodyMass is destructed!" << endl;
  }
};

auto main() -> int
{
  cout << "[unique_ptr_1.cpp]" << endl;
  auto myWeight = make_unique<BodyMass>(1, 165.3f);
  cout << endl << "Doing something!!!" << endl << endl;
  return 0;
}
```

We try to construct a new `unique_ptr` pointer that points to the address that holds a `BodyMass` data type. In `BodyMass`, we have a constructor as well as a destructor. Now, let's see how the `unique_ptr` pointer works by running the preceding code. The output we get on the screen should be like the following screenshot:

```
[unique_ptr_1.cpp]
BodyMass is constructed!
Id = 1
Weight = 165.3

Doing something!!!

BodyMass is destructed!
```

As we can see in the preceding screenshot, the constructor is invoked when we construct `unique_ptr`. Moreover, unlike the traditional C++ language, where we have to free the memory up when we use a pointer, in modern C++, the memory will be freed up automatically when it is out of scope. We can see that the destructor of `BodyMass` is invoked when the program exits, which means `myWeight` is out of scope.

Now, let's test the exclusiveness of `unique_ptr` by analyzing the following code snippet:

```cpp
/* unique_ptr_2.cpp */
#include <memory>
#include <iostream>

using namespace std;
struct BodyMass
{
  int Id;
  float Weight;

  BodyMass(int id, float weight) :
    Id(id),
    Weight(weight)
    {
      cout << "BodyMass is constructed!" << endl;
      cout << "Id = " << Id << endl;
      cout << "Weight = " << Weight << endl;
    }

  BodyMass(const BodyMass &other) :
    Id(other.Id),
    Weight(other.Weight)
    {
      cout << "BodyMass is copy constructed!" << endl;
      cout << "Id = " << Id << endl;
      cout << "Weight = " << Weight << endl;
    }
```

```
    ~BodyMass()
    {
        cout << "BodyMass is destructed!" << endl;
    }
};

auto main() -> int
{
    cout << "[unique_ptr_2.cpp]" << endl;

    auto myWeight = make_unique<BodyMass>(1, 165.3f);

    // The compiler will forbid to create another pointer
    // that points to the same allocated memory/object
    // since it's unique pointer
    //auto myWeight2 = myWeight;

    // However, we can do the following expression
    // since it actually copies the object that has been allocated
    // (not the unique_pointer)
    auto copyWeight = *myWeight;

    return 0;
}
```

As we can see in the preceding code, we see that we can't assign the `unique_ptr` instance to another pointer since it will break the exclusiveness of `unique_ptr`. The compiler will throw an error if we make the following expression:

```
auto myWeight2 = myWeight;
```

However, we can assign the value of the `unique_ptr` to another object since it has been allocated. To prove it, we have added a copy constructor to log when the following expression is executed:

```
auto copyWeight = *myWeight;
```

If we run the preceding `unique_ptr_2.cpp` code, we will see the following output on the screen:

```
Command Prompt                                        —    □    ×
[unique_ptr_2.cpp]
BodyMass is constructed!
Id = 1
Weight = 165.3
BodyMass is copy constructed!
Id = 1
Weight = 165.3
BodyMass is destructed!
BodyMass is destructed!
```

As we can see in the preceding screenshot, the copy constructor is called when the copy assignment is executed. It proves that we can copy the value of the `unique_ptr` object but not the object itself.

As we discussed earlier, `unique_ptr` has moved the constructor, although it has no copy constructor. The use of this construction can be found in the following piece of code:

```cpp
/* unique_ptr_3.cpp */
#include <memory>
#include <iostream>

using namespace std;

struct BodyMass
{
  int Id;
  float Weight;

  BodyMass(int id, float weight) :
    Id(id),
    Weight(weight)
    {
      cout << "BodyMass is constructed!" << endl;
      cout << "Id = " << Id << endl;
      cout << "Weight = " << Weight << endl;
    }

  ~BodyMass()
   {
     cout << "BodyMass is destructed!" << endl;
```

```
      }
};

unique_ptr<BodyMass> GetBodyMass()
{
  return make_unique<BodyMass>(1, 165.3f);
}

unique_ptr<BodyMass> UpdateBodyMass(
  unique_ptr<BodyMass> bodyMass)
  {
    bodyMass->Weight += 1.0f;
    return bodyMass;
  }

auto main() -> int
{
  cout << "[unique_ptr_3.cpp]" << endl;

  auto myWeight = GetBodyMass();

  cout << "Current weight = " << myWeight->Weight << endl;

  myWeight = UpdateBodyMass(move(myWeight));
  cout << "Updated weight = " << myWeight->Weight << endl;

  return 0;
}
```

In the preceding code, we have two new functions--GetBodyMass() and
UpdateBodyMass(). We construct a new unique_ptr object from the GetBodyMass()
function, then we update the value of its *Weight* using the UpdateBodyMass() function. We
can see that we use the move function when we pass an argument to the
UpdateBodyMass() function. It's because unique_ptr has no copy constructor, and it has
to be moved in order to update the value of its property. The screen output of the preceding
code is as follows:

```
[unique_ptr_3.cpp]
BodyMass is constructed!
Id = 1
Weight = 165.3
Current weight = 165.3
Updated weight = 166.3
BodyMass is destructed!
```

Sharing objects using shared_ptr

In contrast to unique_ptr, shared_ptr implements shared ownership semantics, so it offers the ability of copy constructor and copy assignment. Although they have a difference in the implementation, shared_ptr is actually the counted version of unique_ptr. We can call the use_count() method to find out the counter value of the shared_ptr reference. Each instance of the shared_ptr valid object is counted as one. We can copy the shared_ptr instance to other shared_ptr variables and the reference count will be incremented. When a shared_ptr object is destroyed, the destructor decrements the reference count. The object will be deleted only if the count reaches zero. Now let's examine the following shared_ptr code:

```cpp
/* shared_ptr_1.cpp */
#include <memory>
#include <iostream>

using namespace std;

auto main() -> int
{
  cout << "[shared_ptr_1.cpp]" << endl;

  auto sp1 = shared_ptr<int>{};

  if(sp1)
     cout << "sp1 is initialized" << endl;
  else
     cout << "sp1 is not initialized" << endl;
  cout << "sp1 pointing counter = " << sp1.use_count() << endl;
  if(sp1.unique())
     cout << "sp1 is unique" << endl;
  else
    cout << "sp1 is not unique" << endl;
```

```
    cout << endl;
    sp1 = make_shared<int>(1234);
    if(sp1)
      cout << "sp1 is initialized" << endl;
    else
      cout << "sp1 is not initialized" << endl;
    cout << "sp1 pointing counter = " << sp1.use_count() << endl;
    if(sp1.unique())
      cout << "sp1 is unique" << endl;
    else
      cout << "sp1 is not unique" << endl;
    cout << endl;

    auto sp2 = sp1;
    cout << "sp1 pointing counter = " << sp1.use_count() << endl;
    if(sp1.unique())
      cout << "sp1 is unique" << endl;
    else
      cout << "sp1 is not unique" << endl;
    cout << endl;

    cout << "sp2 pointing counter = " << sp2.use_count() << endl;
    if(sp2.unique())
      cout << "sp2 is unique" << endl;
    else
      cout << "sp2 is not unique" << endl;
    cout << endl;

    sp2.reset();

    cout << "sp1 pointing counter = " << sp1.use_count() << endl;
    if(sp1.unique())
      cout << "sp1 is unique" << endl;
    else
      cout << "sp1 is not unique" << endl;
    cout << endl;

    return 0;
}
```

Before we examine each line of the preceding code, let's take a look at the following output that should appear on the console window:

```
[shared_ptr_1.cpp]
sp1 is not initialized
sp1 pointing counter = 0
sp1 is not unique

sp1 is initialized
sp1 pointing counter = 1
sp1 is unique

sp1 pointing counter = 2
sp1 is not unique

sp2 pointing counter = 2
sp2 is not unique

sp1 pointing counter = 1
sp1 is unique
```

First, we create a `shared_ptr` object named `sp1` without instantiating it. From the console, we see that `sp1` is not initialized and the counter is still 0. It is also not unique since the pointer is pointed to nothing. We then construct `sp1` using the `make_shared` method. Now, `sp1` is initialized and the counter becomes 1. It also becomes unique since it's only one of the `shared_ptr` object (proven by the value of the counter that is 1). Next, we create another variable named `sp2`, and copy `sp1` to it. As a result, `sp1` and `sp2` now share the same object proven by the counter and the uniqueness value. Then, invoking the `reset()` method in `sp2` will destroy the object of `sp2`. Now, the counter of `sp1` becomes 1, and it is unique again.

In the `shared_ptr_1.cpp` code, we declare the `unique_ptr` object using `shared_ptr<int>`, then invoke `make_shared<int>` to instance the pointer. It's because we just need to analyze the `shared_ptr` behavior. However, we should use `make_shared<>` for shared pointers since it has to keep the reference counter somewhere in memory and allocates the counter and memory for objects together instead of two separate allocations.

Tracking the objects using a weak_ptr pointer

We have discussed the `shared_ptr` in the preceding section. The pointer is actually a little bit fat pointer. It logically points to two objects, the object being managed and the pointing counter using the `use_count()` method. Every `shared_ptr` basically has a strong reference count that prevents the object from being deleted and a weak reference count that does not prevent the object being deleted if the `shared_ptr` object's use count reaches 0, although we don't even use the weak reference count. For this reason, we can use only one reference count so we can use the `weak_ptr` pointer. The `weak_ptr` pointer refers to an object that is managed by `shared_ptr`. The advantage of `weak_ptr` is that it can be used to refer to an object, but we can only access it if the object still exists and without preventing the object from being deleted by some other reference holder if the strong reference count reaches zero. It is useful when we deal with data structures. Let's take a look at the following block of code to analyze the use of `weak_ptr`:

```cpp
/* weak_ptr_1.cpp */
#include <memory>
#include <iostream>

using namespace std;

auto main() -> int
{
  cout << "[weak_ptr_1.cpp]" << endl;

  auto sp = make_shared<int>(1234);

  auto wp = weak_ptr<int>{ sp };

  if(wp.expired())
   cout << "wp is expired" << endl;
  else
   cout << "wp is not expired" << endl;
  cout << "wp pointing counter = " << wp.use_count() << endl;
  if(auto locked = wp.lock())
   cout << "wp is locked. Value = " << *locked << endl;
  else
  {
    cout << "wp is unlocked" << endl;
    wp.reset();
  }
  cout << endl;

  sp = nullptr;

  if(wp.expired())
```

```
    cout << "wp is expired" << endl;
  else
    cout << "wp is not expired" << endl;
  cout << "wp pointing counter = " << wp.use_count() << endl;
  if(auto locked = wp.lock())
    cout << "wp is locked. Value = " << *locked << endl;
  else
  {
    cout << "wp is unlocked" << endl;
    wp.reset();
  }
  cout << endl;

  return 0;
}
```

Before we analyze the preceding code, let's take a look at the following screenshot from the output console if we run the code:

At first, we instantiate shared_ptr and, as we discussed previously, the weak_ptr points to the object managed by shared_ptr. We then assign wp to the shared_ptr variable, sp. After we have a weak_ptr pointer, we then check its behavior. By calling the expired() method, we can figure out whether the referenced object was already deleted. And, since the wp variable is just constructed, it is not expired yet. The weak_ptr pointer also holds the value of the object counting by calling the use_count() method, as we used in shared_ptr. We then invoke the locked() method to create a shared_ptr that manages the referenced object and finds the value weak_ptr is pointing at. We now have a shared_ptr variable pointing to the address that holds the 1234 value.

We reset `sp` to `nullptr` afterward. Although we don't touch the `weak_ptr` pointer, it is also changed. As we can see from the console screenshot, now `wp` is expired since the object has been deleted. The counter also changes and becomes 0 since it points to nothing. Moreover, it is unlocked since the `shared_ptr` object has been deleted.

Storing many different data types using tuples

We will get acquainted with tuples, an object that is able to hold a collection of elements, and each element can be of a different type. It is a new feature in C++11 and gives power to functional programming. The tuples will be most useful when creating a function that returns the value. Moreover, since functions don't change the global state in functional programming, we can return the tuples for all the values we need to change instead. Now, let's examine the following piece of code:

```cpp
/* tuples_1.cpp */
#include <tuple>
#include <iostream>

using namespace std;

auto main() -> int
{
    cout << "[tuples_1.cpp]" << endl;

    // Initializing two Tuples
    tuple<int, string, bool> t1(1, "Robert", true);
    auto t2 = make_tuple(2, "Anna", false);

    // Displaying t1 Tuple elements
    cout << "t1 elements:" << endl;
    cout << get<0>(t1) << endl;
    cout << get<1>(t1) << endl;
    cout << (get<2>(t1) == true ? "Male" : "Female") << endl;
    cout << endl;

    // Displaying t2 Tuple elements
    cout << "t2 elements:" << endl;
    cout << get<0>(t2) << endl;
    cout << get<1>(t2) << endl;
    cout << (get<2>(t2) == true ? "Male" : "Female") << endl;
    cout << endl;
```

```
    return 0;
}
```

In the preceding code, we created two tuples, t1 and t2, with different constructing techniques using tuple<int, string, bool> and make_tuple. However, these two different techniques will give the same result. Obviously, in the code, we access each element in tuples using get<x>(y), where x is the index and y is the tuple object. And, with confidence, we will get the following result on the console:

Unpacking tuples values

Another useful member that functions in the tuples classes is tie(), which is used to unpack a tuple into individual objects or create a tuple of lvalue references. Also, we have the ignore helper class in tuples, a placeholder to skip an element when unpacking a tuple is using tie(). Let's see the use of tie() and ignore in the following block of code:

```
/* tuples_2.cpp */
#include <tuple>
#include <iostream>

using namespace std;

auto main() -> int
{
    cout << "[tuples_2.cpp]" << endl;

    // Initializing two Tuples
    tuple<int, string, bool> t1(1, "Robert", true);
    auto t2 = make_tuple(2, "Anna", false);
```

```
        int i;
        string s;
        bool b;

        // Unpacking t1 Tuples
        tie(i, s, b) = t1;
        cout << "tie(i, s, b) = t1" << endl;
        cout << "i = " << i << endl;
        cout << "s = " << s << endl;
        cout << "b = " << boolalpha << b << endl;
        cout << endl;

        // Unpacking t2 Tuples
        tie(ignore, s, ignore) = t2;
        cout << "tie(ignore, s, ignore) = t2" << endl;
        cout << "new i = " << i << endl;
        cout << "new s = " << s << endl;
        cout << "new b = " << boolalpha << b << endl;
        cout << endl;

        return 0;
    }
```

In the preceding code, we have the same two tuples that `tuples_1.cpp` has. We want to unpack `t1` into variables `i`, `s`, and `b` respectively, using the `tie()` method. Then, we unpack `t2` to the `s` variable only, ignoring the `int` and `bool` data in `t2`. If we run the code, the output should be as follows:

```
Command Prompt                                            —   □   ✕
[tuples_2.cpp]
tie(i, s, b) = t1
i = 1
s = Robert
b = true

tie(ignore, s, ignore) = t2
new i = 1
new s = Anna
new b = true
```

Returning a tuple value type

As we discussed earlier, we can maximize the use of tuples in functional programming when we want to write a function that returns multiple data. Let's take a look at the following block of code to know how to return the tuple and access the return value:

```cpp
/* tuples_3.cpp */
#include <tuple>
#include <iostream>

using namespace std;

tuple<int, string, bool> GetData(int DataId)
{
  if (DataId == 1)
    return std::make_tuple(0, "Chloe", false);
  else if (DataId == 2)
    return std::make_tuple(1, "Bryan", true);
  else
    return std::make_tuple(2, "Zoey", false);
 }

auto main() -> int
{
  cout << "[tuples_3.cpp]" << endl;

  auto name = GetData(1);
  cout << "Details of Id 1" << endl;
  cout << "ID = " << get<0>(name) << endl;
  cout << "Name = " << get<1>(name) << endl;
  cout << "Gender = " << (get<2>(name) == true ?
    "Male" : "Female");
  cout << endl << endl;

  int i;
  string s;
  bool b;
  tie(i, s, b) = GetData(2);
  cout << "Details of Id 2" << endl;
  cout << "ID = " << i << endl;
  cout << "Name = " << s << endl;
  cout << "Gender = " << (b == true ? "Male" : "Female");
  cout << endl;
  return 0;
}
```

As we can see in the preceding code, we have a new function named `GetData()` returning a `Tuple` value. From that function, we will consume the data returning from it. We begin with creating the name variable and get the value from the `GetData()` function. We can also use the `tie()` method to unpack the tuple coming from the `GetData()` function, as we can see in the code when we access the data when ID = 2. The output on the console should be like the following screenshot when we run the code:

```
[tuples_3.cpp]
Details of Id 1
ID = 0
Name = Chloe
Gender = Female

Details of Id 2
ID = 1
Name = Bryan
Gender = Male
```

Summary

We have refreshed our experience in the C++ language by completing this chapter. Now we know that C++ is more modern, and it comes with numerous features that assist us in creating a better program. We can use the Standard Library to make our code efficient since we don't need to write too many redundant functions. We can use the Lambda expression to make our code tidy, easy to read, and easy to maintain. We can also use the smart pointer so we don't need to worry about memory management anymore. Moreover, as we are concerned about immutability in functional programming, we will discuss that deeper in the next chapter; the use of tuples can help us ensure that no global state is involved in our code.

In the next chapter, we will discuss First-Class and Pure Function, which is used to purify our class and ensure that no outside state is involved in the current function. As a result, it will avoid side effects in our functional code.

2
Manipulating Functions in Functional Programming

In the previous chapter, we talked about modern C++ in depth, especially about the new feature in C++11--the Lambda expression. As we discussed earlier, the Lambda expression is useful in simplifying function notation. Thus, in this chapter, we will apply the power of the Lambda expression again, which will be used in functional code, especially when we talk about currying--the technique to split and reduce the current function.

In this chapter, we will discuss the following topics:

- Applying the first-class function and higher-order function so that our functions can not only be invoked as a function, but also be assigned to any variable, pass a function, and return a function
- Pure function, to avoid side effect in our function since it no longer contacts an outside state
- Currying, as mentioned at the beginning of this chapter, to reduce the multiple arguments function so we can evaluate a sequence of functions, with a single argument in each function

Applying the first-class function in all functions

The first-class function is just a normal class. We can treat the first-class function like any other data type. However, in the language that supports the first-class function, we can do the following tasks without invoking the compiler recursively:

- Passing a function as another function's parameter
- Assigning functions to variables
- Storing functions in collections
- Creating new functions from the existing functions at runtime

Fortunately, C++ can be used to solve the preceding tasks. We will discuss it in depth in the following topics.

Passing a function as another function's parameter

Let's start to pass a function as the function parameter. We will choose one of four functions and invoke the function from its main function. The code will look like this:

```cpp
/* first_class_1.cpp */
#include <functional>
#include <iostream>

using namespace std;

// Defining a type of function named FuncType
// representing a function
// that pass two int arguments
// and return an int value
typedef function<int(int, int)> FuncType;

int addition(int x, int y)
{
  return x + y;
}

int subtraction(int x, int y)
{
  return x - y;
}
```

```cpp
int multiplication(int x, int y)
{
  return x * y;
}

int division(int x, int y)
{
  return x / y;
}

void PassingFunc(FuncType fn, int x, int y)
{
  cout << "Result = " << fn(x, y) << endl;
}

auto main() -> int
{
  cout << "[first_class_1.cpp]" << endl;
  int i, a, b;
  FuncType func;

  // Displaying menu for user
  cout << "Select mode:" << endl;
  cout << "1. Addition" << endl;
  cout << "2. Subtraction" << endl;
  cout << "3. Multiplication" << endl;
  cout << "4. Division" << endl;
  cout << "Choice: ";
  cin >> i;

  // Preventing user to select
  // unavailable modes
  if(i < 1 || i > 4)
  {
     cout << "Please select available mode!";
     return 1;
  }
  // Getting input from user for variable a
  cout << "a -> ";
  cin >> a;

  // Input validation for variable a
  while (cin.fail())
  {
    // Clearing input buffer to restore cin to a usable state
    cin.clear();
    // Ignoring last input
    cin.ignore(INT_MAX, '\n');
```

```
        cout << "You can only enter numbers.\n";
        cout << "Enter a number for variable a -> ";
        cin >> a;
    }

    // Getting input from user for variable b
    cout << "b -> ";
    cin >> b;

    // Input validation for variable b
    while (cin.fail())
    {
        // Clearing input buffer to restore cin to a usable state
        cin.clear();

        // Ignoring last input
        cin.ignore(INT_MAX, '\n');

        cout << "You can only enter numbers.\n";
        cout << "Enter a number for variable b -> ";
        cin >> b;
    }
    switch(i)
    {
        case 1: PassingFunc(addition, a, b); break;
        case 2: PassingFunc(subtraction, a, b); break;
        case 3: PassingFunc(multiplication, a, b); break;
        case 4: PassingFunc(division, a, b); break;
    }

    return 0;
}
```

From the preceding code, we can see that we have four functions, and we want the user to choose one, and then run it. In the switch statement, we will invoke one of the four functions based on the choice of the user. We will pass the selected function to `PassingFunc()`, as we can see in the following code snippet:

```
case 1: PassingFunc(addition, a, b); break;
case 2: PassingFunc(subtraction, a, b); break;
case 3: PassingFunc(multiplication, a, b); break;
case 4: PassingFunc(division, a, b); break;
```

We also have the input validation to prevent the user from selecting unavailable modes as well as inputting a non-integer value for variable a and b. The output we will see on the screen should look like this:

```
Select Command Prompt                              —    □    ×
[first_class_1.cpp]
Select mode:
1. Addition
2. Subtraction
3. Multiplication
4. Division
Choice: 3
a -> r
You can only enter numbers.
Enter a number for variable a -> e
You can only enter numbers.
Enter a number for variable a -> 4
b -> 2
Result = 8
```

The preceding screenshot shows that we select the Multiplication mode from the available modes. Then, we try to input the r and e variables for variable a. Fortunately, the program rejects it since we have had the input validation. Then, we give 4 to variable a and 2 to variable b. As we expect, the program gives us 8 as a result.

As we can see in the first_class_1.cpp program, we use the std::function class and the typedef keyword to simplify the code. The std::function class is used to store, copy, and invoke any callable functions, Lambda expressions, or other function objects, as well as pointers to member functions and pointers to data members. However, the typedef keyword is used as an alias name for another type or function.

Assigning a function to a variable

We can also assign a function to the variable so we can call the function by calling the variable. We will refactor first_class_1.cpp, and it will be as follows:

```cpp
/* first_class_2.cpp */
#include <functional>
#include <iostream>
using namespace std;

// Defining a type of function named FuncType
// representing a function
// that pass two int arguments
// and return an int value
typedef function<int(int, int)> FuncType;
```

```cpp
int addition(int x, int y)
{
  return x + y;
}

int subtraction(int x, int y)
{
  return x - y;
}

int multiplication(int x, int y)
{
  return x * y;
}

int division(int x, int y)
{
  return x / y;
}

auto main() -> int
{
  cout << "[first_class_2.cpp]" << endl;

  int i, a, b;
  FuncType func;

  // Displaying menu for user
  cout << "Select mode:" << endl;
  cout << "1. Addition" << endl;
  cout << "2. Subtraction" << endl;
  cout << "3. Multiplication" << endl;
  cout << "4. Division" << endl;
  cout << "Choice: ";
  cin >> i;

  // Preventing user to select
  // unavailable modes
  if(i < 1 || i > 4)
  {
    cout << "Please select available mode!";
    return 1;
  }

  // Getting input from user for variable a
  cout << "a -> ";
  cin >> a;
```

```
  // Input validation for variable a
  while (cin.fail())
  {
    // Clearing input buffer to restore cin to a usable state
    cin.clear();

    // Ignoring last input
    cin.ignore(INT_MAX, '\n');

    cout << "You can only enter numbers.\n";
    cout << "Enter a number for variable a -> ";
    cin >> a;
  }

  // Getting input from user for variable b
  cout << "b -> ";
  cin >> b;

  // Input validation for variable b
  while (cin.fail())
  {
    // Clearing input buffer to restore cin to a usable state
    cin.clear();

    // Ignoring last input
    cin.ignore(INT_MAX, '\n');

    cout << "You can only enter numbers.\n";
    cout << "Enter a number for variable b -> ";
    cin >> b;
  }

  switch(i)
  {
    case 1: func = addition; break;
    case 2: func = subtraction; break;
    case 3: func = multiplication; break;
    case 4: func = division; break;
  }
  cout << "Result = " << func(a, b) << endl;

  return 0;
}
```

We will now assign the four functions based on the user's choice and store the selected function in the `func` variable inside the switch statement as follows:

```
case 1: func = addition; break;
case 2: func = subtraction; break;
case 3: func = multiplication; break;
case 4: func = division; break;
```

After the `func` variable is assigned with the user's choice, the code will just call the variable like it calls the function, as shown in the following line of code:

```
cout << "Result = " << func(a, b) << endl;
```

And we will then obtain the same output on the console if we run the code.

Storing a function in the container

Now, let's save the function to the container. Here, we will use **vector** as the container. The code is written as follows:

```
/* first_class_3.cpp */
#include <vector>
#include <functional>
#include <iostream>

using namespace std;

// Defining a type of function named FuncType
// representing a function
// that pass two int arguments
// and return an int value
typedef function<int(int, int)> FuncType;

int addition(int x, int y)
{
    return x + y;
}

int subtraction(int x, int y)
{
    return x - y;
}

int multiplication(int x, int y)
{
    return x * y;
```

```cpp
}

int division(int x, int y)
{
  return x / y;
}

auto main() -> int
{
  cout << "[first_class_3.cpp]" << endl;

  // Declaring a vector containing FuncType element
  vector<FuncType> functions;

  // Assigning several FuncType elements to the vector
  functions.push_back(addition);
  functions.push_back(subtraction);
  functions.push_back(multiplication);
  functions.push_back(division);

  int i, a, b;
  function<int(int, int)> func;

  // Displaying menu for user
  cout << "Select mode:" << endl;
  cout << "1. Addition" << endl;
  cout << "2. Subtraction" << endl;
  cout << "3. Multiplication" << endl;
  cout << "4. Division" << endl;
  cout << "Choice: ";
  cin >> i;

  // Preventing user to select
  // unavailable modes
  if(i < 1 || i > 4)
  {
    cout << "Please select available mode!";
    return 1;
  }

  // Getting input from user for variable a
  cout << "a -> ";
  cin >> a;

  // Input validation for variable a
  while (cin.fail())
  {
    // Clearing input buffer to restore cin to a usable state
```

```
        cin.clear();

        // Ignoring last input
        cin.ignore(INT_MAX, '\n');

        cout << "You can only enter numbers.\n";
        cout << "Enter a number for variable a -> ";
        cin >> a;
    }

    // Getting input from user for variable b
    cout << "b -> ";
    cin >> b;

    // Input validation for variable b
    while (cin.fail())
    {
        // Clearing input buffer to restore cin to a usable state
        cin.clear();

        // Ignoring last input
        cin.ignore(INT_MAX, '\n');

        cout << "You can only enter numbers.\n";
        cout << "Enter a number for variable b -> ";
        cin >> b;
    }

    // Invoking the function inside the vector
    cout << "Result = " << functions.at(i - 1)(a, b) << endl;

    return 0;
}
```

From the preceding code, we can see that we create a new vector named functions, then store four different functions to it. Just like we did with our two previous code examples, we ask the user to select the mode as well. However, now the code becomes simpler, since we don't need to add the switch statement; we can select the function directly by selecting the vector index, as we can see in the following code snippet:

```
cout << "Result = " << functions.at(i - 1)(a, b) << endl;
```

However, since the vector is a **zero-based** index, we have to adjust the index with the menu choice. The result will be same with our two previous code samples.

Creating a new function from the existing functions at runtime

Now let's make a new function at runtime from the preexisting functions. Let's suppose we have two collections of functions, the first is hyperbolic functions and the second is the inverse of the first one. Beside these built-in functions, we also add one user-defined function to calculate the squared number in the first collection and the inverse of the squared number in the second collection. Then, we will implement the function composition and build a new function from two existing functions.

 Function composition is a process to combine two or more simple functions to create a more complex one. The result of each function is passed as the argument to the next function. The final result is obtained from the last function result. In a mathematical approach, we usually use the following notation to function composition: `compose(f, g) (x) = f(g(x))`. Let's suppose we have the following code:
`double x, y, z; // ... y = g(x); z = f(y);`

So, to simplify the notation, we can use the function composition and have the following notation for z:

`z = f(g(x));`

If we run the hyperbolic functions, then pass the result to the inverse one, we will see that we indeed get the original value that we passed to the hyperbolic function. Now, let's take a look at the following code:

```
/* first_class_4.cpp */
#include <vector>
#include <cmath>
#include <algorithm>
#include <functional>
#include <iostream>

using std::vector;
using std::function;
using std::transform;
using std::back_inserter;
using std::cout;
using std::endl;

// Defining a type of function named HyperbolicFunc
// representing a function
// that pass a double argument
```

```cpp
// and return an double value
typedef function<double(double)> HyperbolicFunc;

// Initializing a vector containing four functions
vector<HyperbolicFunc> funcs = {
  sinh,
  cosh,
  tanh,
  [](double x) {
    return x*x; }
};

// Initializing a vector containing four functions
vector<HyperbolicFunc> inverseFuncs = {
  asinh,
  acosh,
  atanh,
  [](double x) {
    return exp(log(x)/2); }
};

// Declaring a template to be able to be reused
template <typename A, typename B, typename C>
function<C(A)> compose(
  function<C(B)> f,
  function<B(A)> g) {
    return [f,g](A x) {
      return f(g(x));
  };
}

auto main() -> int
{
  cout << "[first_class_4.cpp]" << endl;

  // Declaring a template to be able to be reused
  vector<HyperbolicFunc> composedFuncs;

  // Initializing a vector containing several double elements
  vector<double> nums;
  for (int i = 1; i <= 5; ++i)
    nums.push_back(i * 0.2);

  // Transforming the element inside the vector
  transform(
    begin(inverseFuncs),
    end(inverseFuncs),
    begin(funcs),
```

```
      back_inserter(composedFuncs),
      compose<double, double, double>);

   for (auto num: nums)
   {
      for (auto func: composedFuncs)
         cout << "f(g(" << num << ")) = " << func(num) << endl;

      cout << "--------------" << endl;
   }

   return 0;
}
```

As we can see in the preceding code, we have two function collections--`funcs` and `inverseFuncs`. Moreover, as we discussed previously, the `inverseFuncs` function is the inverse of the `funcs` function. The `funcs` function contains three built-in hyperbolic functions, along with one user-defined function to calculate the squared number, whereas `inverseFuncs` contains three built-in inverse hyperbolic functions along with one user-defined function to compute the inverse of the squared number.

> As we can see in the preceding `first_class_4.cpp` code, we will use individual classes/functions when calling the `using` keyword. Compared to the other code samples in this chapter, the use of the `using` keyword in individual classes/functions is inconsistent, since we use `using namespace std`. It's because there's a clashing function name in the `std` namespace, so we have to call them individually.

By using these two collections of functions, we will construct one new function from them. To achieve this purpose, we will use the `transform()` function to combine the two functions from the two different collections. The code snippet is as follows:

```
transform(
   begin(inverseFuncs),
   inverseFuncs.end(inverseFuncs),
   begin(funcs),
   back_inserter(composedFuncs),
   compose<double, double, double>);
```

Now, we have a new function collection stored in the `composedFuncs` vector. We can iterate the collection and pass the value we have provided in the `nums` variable to this new function. We should obtain the following output on the console if we run the code:

```
Command Prompt                                    —    □    ×
[first_class_4.cpp]
f(g(0.2)) = 0.2
f(g(0.2)) = 0.2
f(g(0.2)) = 0.2
f(g(0.2)) = 0.2
---------------
f(g(0.4)) = 0.4
f(g(0.4)) = 0.4
f(g(0.4)) = 0.4
f(g(0.4)) = 0.4
---------------
f(g(0.6)) = 0.6
f(g(0.6)) = 0.6
f(g(0.6)) = 0.6
f(g(0.6)) = 0.6
---------------
f(g(0.8)) = 0.8
f(g(0.8)) = 0.8
f(g(0.8)) = 0.8
f(g(0.8)) = 0.8
---------------
f(g(1)) = 1
f(g(1)) = 1
f(g(1)) = 1
f(g(1)) = 1
---------------
```

As we can see from the preceding output, whatever we pass to the transforming function, we will get the same output as the input. Here, we can prove that C++ programming can be used to compose a function from two or more existing functions.

 On the preceding `first_class_4.cpp` code, we use `template<>` in the code. If you need a more detailed explanation about `template<>`, refer to `Chapter 7`, *Running Parallel Execution Using Concurrency*.

Getting acquainted with three functional techniques in the higher-order function

We discussed that in the first-class function, the C++ language treats the functions as the value, which means we can pass them to the other functions, assign to variables, and so on. However, we have another term in functional programming, that is, a higher-order function, which are functions that work on other functions. It means the higher-order function can pass functions as the argument and can also return a function.

The higher-order function concept can be applied to the function in general, like in a mathematical function, instead of the first-class function concept that can only be applied in the functional programming language. Now, let's examine the three most useful higher-order functions in functional programming--**map**, **filter**, and **fold**.

Executing each element list using map

We won't talk about map as a container in the C++ language, but a feature in the higher-order function instead. This feature is used to apply a given function to each element of the list and return a list of results in the same order. We can use the `transform()` function to achieve this purpose. As you know, we already discussed this function previously. However, we can take a look at the following piece of code to view the use of the `transform()` function:

```
/* transform_1.cpp */
#include <vector>
#include <algorithm>
#include <iostream>

using namespace std;

auto main() -> int
{
  cout << "[transform_1.cpp]" << endl;

  // Initializing a vector containing integer element
  vector<int> v1;
  for (int i = 0; i < 5; ++i)
    v1.push_back(i);

  // Creating another v2 vector
  vector<int> v2;
  // Resizing the size of v2 exactly same with v1
```

```
    v2.resize(v1.size());

    // Transforming the element inside the vector
    transform (
      begin(v1),
      end(v1),
      begin(v2),
      [](int i){
        return i * i;});

    // Displaying the elements of v1
    std::cout << "v1 contains:";
    for (auto v : v1)
      std::cout << " " << v;
    std::cout << endl;

    // Displaying the elements of v2
    std::cout << "v2 contains:";
    for (auto v : v2)
      std::cout << " " << v;
    std::cout << endl;

    return 0;
}
```

As shown in our preceding definition of map in the higher-order function, it will apply the given function to each element of the list. In the preceding code, we try to map the v1 vector to the v2 vector with the given function in the Lambda expression as follows:

```
transform (
  begin(v1),
  end(v1),
  begin(v2),
  [](int i){
    return i * i;});
```

If we run the code, we should get the following output on the console screen:

```
Command Prompt                                                    —    □    ×
[transform_1.cpp]
v1 contains: 0 1 2 3 4
v2 contains: 0 1 4 9 16
```

As we can see in the output display, we transform v1 into v2 using the given function notating in the Lambda expression, which is doubling the input value.

Extracting data using filter

Filter, in a higher-order function, is a function to produce a new data structure from the existing one that exactly matches each element in the new data structure to a given predicate returning a Boolean value. In C++ language, we can apply the copy_if() function, which is added in C++11, to gain the filtering processes. Let's take a look at the following piece of code to analyze the filtering process using the copy_if() function:

```cpp
/* filter_1.cpp */
#include <vector>
#include <algorithm>
#include <iterator>
#include <iostream>

using namespace std;

auto main() -> int
{
  cout << "[filter_1.cpp]" << endl;

  // Initializing a vector containing integer elements
  vector<int> numbers;
  for (int i = 0; i < 20; ++i)
    numbers.push_back(i);

  // Displaying the elements of numbers
  cout << "The original numbers: " << endl;
  copy(
   begin(numbers),
   end(numbers),
   ostream_iterator<int>(cout, " "));
  cout << endl;

  // Declaring a vector containing int elements
  vector<int> primes;

  // Filtering the vector
  copy_if(
    begin(numbers),
    end(numbers),
    back_inserter(primes),
    [](int n) {
```

```
            if(n < 2) {
                return (n != 0) ? true : false;}
            else {
                for (int j = 2; j < n; ++j) {
                    if (n % j == 0){
                        return false;}
                }

                return true;
            }});

        // Displaying the elements of primes
        // using copy() function
        cout << "The primes numbers: " << endl;
        copy(
          begin(primes),
          end(primes),
          ostream_iterator<int>(cout, " "));
        cout << endl;

        return 0;
    }
```

As we see in the preceding code, we filter the numbers vector into the 0 primes vector using the copy_if() function. We will pass the Lambda expression to decide whether or not the selected element is a prime number, as we used for the lambda_multiline_func.cpp code in Chapter 1, *Diving into Modern C++*. We will also use the copy() function to copy all elements in the selected vector to be printed. The result, when we run the preceding code, should be like this:

```
[filter_1.cpp]
The original numbers:
0 1 2 3 4 5 6 7 8 9 10 11 12 13 14 15 16 17 18 19
The primes numbers:
1 2 3 5 7 11 13 17 19
```

Beside the `copy_if()` function, we can also use the `remove_copy_if()` function to filter the data structure. Instead of selecting the match predicate element from the existing data structure, using the `remove_copy_if()` function will omit the match predicate element, choose the unmatch one, and store it in the new data structure. Let's refactor our `filter_1.cpp` code and create a new vector that is not a prime number. The code will be as follows:

```cpp
/* filter_2.cpp */
#include <vector>
#include <algorithm>
#include <iterator>
#include <iostream>

using namespace std;

int main()
{
    cout << "[filter_2.cpp]" << endl;

    // Initializing a vector containing integer elements
    vector<int> numbers;
    for (int i = 0; i < 20; ++i)
        numbers.push_back(i);

    // Displaying the elements of numbers
    cout << "The original numbers: " << endl;
    copy(
        begin(numbers),
        end(numbers),
        ostream_iterator<int>(cout, " "));
    cout << endl;

    // Declaring a vector containing int elements
    vector<int> nonPrimes;

    // Filtering the vector
    remove_copy_if(
        numbers.begin(),
        numbers.end(),
        back_inserter(nonPrimes),
        [](int n) {
            if(n < 2){
                return (n != 0) ? true : false;}
            else {
                for (int j = 2; j < n; ++j){
                    if (n % j == 0) {
                        return false;}
```

```
        }

        return true;
    }});

    // Displaying the elements of nonPrimes
    // using copy() function
    cout << "The non-primes numbers: " << endl;
    copy(
        begin(nonPrimes),
        end(nonPrimes),
        ostream_iterator<int>(cout, " "));
    cout << endl;

    return 0;
}
```

As we can see from the preceding highlighted code, we refactor the previous code and use the `remove_copy_if()` function to choose non-prime numbers. As we expect, the console window will display the following output:

```
[filter_2.cpp]
The original numbers:
0 1 2 3 4 5 6 7 8 9 10 11 12 13 14 15 16 17 18 19
The non-primes numbers:
0 4 6 8 9 10 12 14 15 16 18
```

We now have the non-prime number instead of the prime number, like we have in the `filter_1.cpp` code.

Combining all elements of a list using fold

In functional programming, a fold is a technique to reduce a data structure into a single value. There are two types of fold--left fold (`foldl`) and right fold (`foldr`). Let's suppose we have a list that contains 0, 1, 2, 3, and 4. Let's use the fold technique to add all the contents of the list, first using `foldl` and then `foldr`. However, there is a significant difference between the two--`foldl` is the left associative, which means we combine the leftmost element then move towards the rightmost element. For instance, by the list we have, we will get the following parentheses:

```
((((0 + 1) + 2) + 3) + 4)
```

While `foldr` is the right associative, which means we will combine the rightmost element then move towards the leftmost element. The parentheses will be like the following line of code:

```
(0 + (1 + (2 + (3 + 4))))
```

Now, let's take a look at the following code:

```cpp
/* fold_1.cpp */
#include <vector>
#include <numeric>
#include <functional>
#include <iostream>

using namespace std;

auto main() -> int
{
  cout << "[fold_1.cpp]" << endl;

  // Initializing a vector containing integer elements
  vector<int> numbers = {0, 1, 2, 3, 4};

  // Calculating the sum of the value
  // in the vector
  auto foldl = accumulate(
    begin(numbers),
    end(numbers),
    0,
    std::plus<int>());

  // Calculating the sum of the value
  // in the vector
  auto foldr = accumulate(
    rbegin(numbers),
    rend(numbers),
    0,
    std::plus<int>());

  // Displaying the calculating result
  cout << "foldl result = " << foldl << endl;
  cout << "foldr result = " << foldr << endl;

  return 0;
}
```

In C++ programming, we can apply the `fold` technique using the `accumulate()` function. As we can see in the preceding code, we use the forward iterator in `foldl` while we use the backward iterator in `foldr`. The output on the console should be like following screenshot:

```
Select Command Prompt                          —    □    ×
[fold_1.cpp]
foldl result = 10
foldr result = 10
```

As we can see in the preceding output screenshot, we've got the same result for both, the `foldl` and `foldr` techniques. For those curious about the order of the sum, we can refactor the preceding code into the following one:

```cpp
/* fold_2.cpp */
#include <vector>
#include <numeric>
#include <functional>
#include <iostream>

using namespace std;

// Function for logging the flow
int addition(const int& x, const int& y)
{
    cout << x << " + " << y << endl;
    return x + y;
}

int main()
{
    cout << "[fold_2.cpp]" << endl;

    // Initializing a vector containing integer elements
    vector<int> numbers = {0, 1, 2, 3, 4};

    // Calculating the sum of the value
    // in the vector
    // from left to right
    cout << "foldl" << endl;
    auto foldl = accumulate(
        begin(numbers),
        end(numbers),
        0,
        addition);
```

```cpp
        // Calculating the sum of the value
        // in the vector
        // from right to left
        cout << endl << "foldr" << endl;
        auto foldr = accumulate(
            rbegin(numbers),
            rend(numbers),
            0,
            addition);

        cout << endl;

        // Displaying the calculating result
        cout << "foldl result = " << foldl << endl;
        cout << "foldr result = " << foldr << endl;

        return 0;
    }
```

In the preceding code, we pass a new `addition()` function and pass it to the `accumulate()` function. From the `addition()` function, we will track the operation of each element. Now, let's run the preceding code whose the output will be as follows:

```
[fold_2.cpp]
foldl
0 + 0
0 + 1
1 + 2
3 + 3
6 + 4

foldr
0 + 4
4 + 3
7 + 2
9 + 1
10 + 0

foldl result = 10
foldr result = 10
```

From the preceding output screenshot, we can see that, even though both `foldl` and `foldr` give the exact same result, they make a different operation order. Since we set the initial value to `0`, the addition operation starts by adding `0` to the first element in the `foldl` technique and to the last element in the `foldr` technique.

We will set the initial value to 0 because 0 is the additive identity that won't impact the addition result. However, in multiplication, we have to consider changing the initial value to 1 since 1 is the identity element for multiplication.

Avoiding the side effect with pure function

A **pure function** is a function that will always return the same result every time it is given the same input. The result doesn't depend on any information or state and won't produce a **side effect**, or a change of the system state outside of the function. Let's take a look at the following piece of code:

```cpp
/* pure_function_1.cpp */
#include <iostream>

using namespace std;

float circleArea(float r)
{
  return 3.14 * r * r;
}

auto main() -> int
{
  cout << "[pure_function_1.cpp]" << endl;

  // Initializing a float variable
  float f = 2.5f;

  // Invoking the circleArea() function
  // passing the f variable five times
  for(int i = 1; i <= 5; ++i)
  {
    cout << "Invocation " << i << " -> ";
    cout << "Result of circleArea(" << f << ") = ";
    cout << circleArea(f) << endl;
  }

  return 0;
}
```

From the preceding code, we can see that we have a function named `circleArea()` to calculate the area of a circle based on the given radius. We then invoke the function five times and pass the same radius value. The output on the console should be like the following screenshot:

```
Command Prompt                                    —    □    ×
[pure_function_1.cpp]
Invocation 1 -> Result of circleArea(2.5) = 19.625
Invocation 2 -> Result of circleArea(2.5) = 19.625
Invocation 3 -> Result of circleArea(2.5) = 19.625
Invocation 4 -> Result of circleArea(2.5) = 19.625
Invocation 5 -> Result of circleArea(2.5) = 19.625
```

As we can see, in five invocations passing the same input, the function returns the same output as well. So that we can say that `circleArea()` is a pure function. Now, let's see how the impure function looks like in the following piece of code:

```cpp
/* impure_function_1.cpp */
#include <iostream>

using namespace std;

// Initializing a global variable
int currentState = 0;

int increment(int i)
{
  currentState += i;
  return currentState;
}

auto main() -> int
{
  cout << "[impure_function_1.cpp]" << endl;

  // Initializing a local variable
  int fix = 5;

  // Involving the global variable
  // in the calculation
  for(int i = 1; i <= 5; ++i)
  {
    cout << "Invocation " << i << " -> ";
    cout << "Result of increment(" << fix << ") = ";
```

```
        cout << increment(fix) << endl;
    }

    return 0;
}
```

In the preceding code, we see that a function named `increment()` increases the value of the `currentState` variable. As we can see, the `increment()` function depends on the value of the `currentState` variable, so it's not a pure function. Let's prove it by running the preceding code. The console window should display the following screenshot:

```
Command Prompt                                          —    □    ×
[impure_function_1.cpp]
Invocation 1 -> Result of increment(5) = 5
Invocation 2 -> Result of increment(5) = 10
Invocation 3 -> Result of increment(5) = 15
Invocation 4 -> Result of increment(5) = 20
Invocation 5 -> Result of increment(5) = 25
```

We see that the `increment()` function gives a different result even though we pass the same input. It's the side effect of the impure function when it depends on the outside state or changes the value of the outside state.

We have been able to distinguish the pure function over the impure function. However, consider the following code:

```cpp
/* im_pure_function_1.cpp */
#include <iostream>

using namespace std;

// Initializing a global variable
float phi = 3.14f;

float circleArea(float r)
{
    return phi * r * r;
}

auto main() -> int
{
    cout << "[im_pure_function_1.cpp]" << endl;

    // Initializing a float variable
```

```
    float f = 2.5f;

    // Involving the global variable
    // in the calculation
    for(int i = 1; i <= 5; ++i)
    {
      cout << "Invocation " << i << " -> ";
      cout << "Result of circleArea(" << f << ") = ";
      cout << circleArea(f) << endl;
    }

    return 0;
}
```

The preceding code comes from pure_function_1.cpp, but we add a global state, phi. If we run the preceding code, we will definitely obtain the same result as pure_function_1.cpp. Although the function returns the same result in the five invocations, circleArea() in im_pure_function_1.cpp is not a pure function since it depends on the phi variable.

> The side effect is not only the change of global state that is done by the function. Printing to the screen is also the side effect. However, since we need to show the result of every code we create, we cannot avoid the existence of printing to screen in our codes. In the next chapter, we will also discuss the immutable state, which is the way we can turn an impure function into a pure function.

Reducing a multiple arguments function with currying

Currying is a technique to split a function that takes multiple arguments into evaluating a sequence of functions, each with a single argument. In other words, we create other functions based on a current function by reducing the current function. Let's suppose we have a function named areaOfRectangle(), which takes two parameters, length and width. The code will be like this:

```
/* curry_1.cpp */

#include <functional>
#include <iostream>

using namespace std;
```

```
// Variadic template for currying
template<typename Func, typename... Args>
auto curry(Func func, Args... args)
{
  return [=](auto... lastParam)
  {
    return func(args..., lastParam...);
  };
}

int areaOfRectangle(int length, int width)
{
  return length * width;
}

auto main() -> int
{
  cout << "[curry_1.cpp]" << endl;

  // Currying the areaOfRectangle() function
  auto length5 = curry(areaOfRectangle, 5);

  // Invoking the curried function
  cout << "Curried with spesific length = 5" << endl;
  for(int i = 0; i <= 5; ++i)
  {
    cout << "length5(" << i << ") = ";
    cout << length5(i) << endl;
  }

  return 0;
}
```

As we can see in the preceding code, we have a variadic template and function named `curry`. We will use this template to construct a currying function. In a normal function invocation, we can invoke the `areaOfRectangle()` function as follows:

```
int i = areaOfRectangle(5, 2);
```

As we can see in the preceding code snippet, we pass 5 and 2 as the argument to the `areaOfRectangle()` function. However, using the curried function, we can reduce the `areaOfRectangle()` function so we just have a single argument. All we have to do is invoke the curry function template as follows:

```
auto length5 = curry(areaOfRectangle, 5);
```

Now, we have the `areaOfRectangle()` function having the value for the `length` argument named `length5`. It's easier for us to call the function and add just the `width` argument as the following code snippet:

`length5(i)` // where i is the width parameter we want to pass

Let's take a look at the output we will see on the console when we run the preceding code:

```
Command Prompt                                          —    □    ×
[curry_1.cpp]
Curried with spesific length = 5
length5(0) = 0
length5(1) = 5
length5(2) = 10
length5(3) = 15
length5(4) = 20
```

The variadic template and function has helped us reduce the `areaOfRectangle()` function to become the `length5()` function. However, it can also help us reduce the function that has more than two arguments. Let's suppose we have a function named `volumeOfRectanglular()` that passes three arguments. We will reduce the function as well, as shown in the following code:

```cpp
/* curry_2.cpp */

#include <functional>
#include <iostream>

using namespace std;

// Variadic template for currying
template<typename Func, typename... Args>
auto curry(Func func, Args... args)
{
  return [=](auto... lastParam)
  {
    return func(args..., lastParam...);
  };
}

int volumeOfRectanglular(
  int length,
  int width,
  int height)
  {
```

```
      return length * width * height;
  }

auto main() -> int
{
  cout << "[curry_2.cpp]" << endl;

  // Currying the volumeOfRectanglular() function
  auto length5width4 = curry(volumeOfRectanglular, 5, 4);

  // Invoking the curried function
  cout << "Curried with spesific data:" << endl;
  cout << "length = 5, width 4" << endl;
  for(int i = 0; i <= 5; ++i)
  {
    cout << "length5width4(" << i << ") = ";
    cout << length5width4(i) << endl;
  }

  return 0;
}
```

As we can see in the preceding code, we have successfully passed the `length` and `width` arguments to the `volumeOfRectanglular()` function only, then reduced it as `length5width4()`. We can invoke the `length5width4()` function and just pass the rest argument, `height`, to it. The following is the output we will see on the console screen if we run the preceding code:

```
Command Prompt                                    —    □    ×
[curry_2.cpp]
Curried with spesific data:
length = 5, width 4
length5width4(0) = 0
length5width4(1) = 20
length5width4(2) = 40
length5width4(3) = 60
length5width4(4) = 80
length5width4(5) = 100
```

By using the currying technique, we can partially evaluate a multiple arguments function by reducing the function so it will only pass a single parameter.

Summary

We have discussed that there are some techniques to manipulate a function. We will gain many advantages from it. Since we can implement the first-class function in the C++ language, we can pass a function as another function's parameter. We can treat a function as a data object so we can assign it to a variable and store it in the container. Also, we can compose a new function from the existing one. Moreover, by using map, filter, and fold, we can implement the higher-order function in every function we create.

Another technique we have to implement in gaining a better functional code is a pure function to avoid a side effect. We can refactor all the functions we have so it won't talk to outside variables or states and won't change and retrieve the value from the outside state. Also, to reduce the multiple arguments function so we can evaluate its sequence, we can implement the currying technique to our function.

In the next chapter, we will discuss another technique to avoid side effects. We will make all states in our code immutable so there's no state that will mutate each time the function is invoked.

3
Applying Immutable State to the Function

After discussing the first-class function and pure function in the previous chapter, now let's talk about a mutable and immutable object. As you have learned, we have to be able to pass a function to another function in a first-class function and ensure that the function returns the same value if we pass the same argument as well. The immutable object, which we will discuss, can help us make these two functional programming concepts available in our code. The topics we will discuss in this chapter are as follows:

- Modifying the variable in a functional programming approach
- Demonstrating the use of const keyword to avoid value modification
- Applying first-class and pure functions to immutable objects
- Refactoring the mutable object into an immutable object
- The benefit of an immutable object over a mutable one

Understanding the essential part from immutable object

In object-oriented programming, we usually manipulate the variable objects many times, even inside the class itself, which we usually describe as the attributes. Also, we sometimes change the global variable from the specific function. However, to gain the immutability feature in functional programming, there are two rules we have to obey. First, we are not allowed to change the local variable. Second, we have to avoid the involvement of the global variable in the function since it will affect the function result.

Modifying a local variable

When we talk about a variable, we are talking about a container to store our data. In our daily programming, we usually reuse the variable we have created. To make it clear, let's take a look at the `mutable_1.cpp` code. We have the `mutableVar` variable and store `100` to it. We then manipulate its value for the `i` variable iteration. The code is written as follows:

```cpp
/* mutable_1.cpp */
#include <iostream>

using namespace std;

auto main() -> int
{
  cout << "[mutable_1.cpp]" << endl;

  // Initializing an int variable
  int mutableVar = 100;
  cout << "Initial mutableVar = " << mutableVar;
  cout << endl;

  // Manipulating mutableVar
  for(int i = 0; i <= 10; ++i)
    mutableVar = mutableVar + i;

  // Displaying mutableVar value
  cout << "After manipulating mutableVar = " << mutableVar;
  cout << endl;

  return 0;
}
```

The result we should see on the screen will be like the following screenshot:

```
C:\WINDOWS\system32\cmd.exe                         —    □    ×
[mutable_1.cpp]
Initial mutableVar = 100
After manipulating mutableVar = 155
```

As we can see, we have successfully manipulated the `mutableVar` variable. However, we treat the `mutableVar` variable as a mutable object. It's because we reuse the `mutableVar` variable many times. In other words, we have broken the immutable rule we discussed earlier. We can, if we want, refactor the `mutable_1.cpp` code to be the immutable one. Let's analyze the `immutable_1.cpp` code. Here, we will create a new local variable each time we intend to change the previous variable. The code is written as follows:

```cpp
/* immutable_1.cpp */
#include <iostream>

using namespace std;

auto main() -> int
{
  cout << "[immutable_1.cpp]" << endl;

  // Initializing an int variable
  int mutableVar = 100;
  cout << "Initial mutableVar = " << mutableVar;
  cout << endl;

  // Manipulating mutableVar using immutable approach
  int mutableVar0 = mutableVar + 0;
  int mutableVar1 = mutableVar0 + 1;
  int mutableVar2 = mutableVar1 + 2;
  int mutableVar3 = mutableVar2 + 3;
  int mutableVar4 = mutableVar3 + 4;
  int mutableVar5 = mutableVar4 + 5;
  int mutableVar6 = mutableVar5 + 6;
  int mutableVar7 = mutableVar6 + 7;
  int mutableVar8 = mutableVar7 + 8;
  int mutableVar9 = mutableVar8 + 9;
  int mutableVar10 = mutableVar9 + 10;

  // Displaying mutableVar value in mutable variable
  cout << "After manipulating mutableVar = " << mutableVar10;
  cout << endl;

  return 0;
}
```

As we can see, to avoid changing the local variable, `mutableVar`, we create the other ten local variables. The result is stored in the `mutableVar10` variable. We then show the result to the console. Indeed, it's uncommon in our programming activities habit. However, this is the way we can do to get the immutable object. By doing this immutable approach, we never miss the previous state since we have all states. Also, the output we get by running `immutable_1.cpp` is completely the same as the output from the `mutable_1.cpp` code, as we can see in the following screenshot:

```
C:\WINDOWS\system32\cmd.exe                              —    □    ×
[immutable_1.cpp]
Initial mutableVar = 100
After manipulating mutableVar = 155
```

However, since we have more code lines in `immutable_1.cpp` compared to the `mutable_1.cpp` code, the performance of the `immutable_1.cpp` code will be slower than the `mutable_1.cpp` code. In addition, of course, the `mutable_1.cpp` code is more efficient than the `immutable_1.cpp` code.

Modifying a variable passed into a function

Now, we will talk about modifying the variable when it is passed to a function. Let's suppose we have a variable named n that contains a string data. We then pass it as a parameter to a function named `Modify()`. Inside the function, we manipulate the name variable. Let's take a look at the following `immutable_2.cpp` code and analyze it:

```cpp
/* immutable_2.cpp */
#include <iostream>

using namespace std;

void Modify(string name)
{
  name = "Alexis Andrews";
}

auto main() -> int
{
  cout << "[immutable_2.cpp]" << endl;

  // Initializing a string variable
  string n = "Frankie Kaur";
```

```
   cout << "Initial name = " << n;
   cout << endl;

   // Invoking Modify() function
   // to modify the n variable
   Modify(n);

   // Displaying n value
   cout << "After manipulating = " << n;
   cout << endl;

   return 0;
}
```

From the preceding code, we see that we store Frankie Kaur as the initial value of the n variable, then modify into Alexis Andrews inside the Modify() function. Now, let's see the output on the screen when we run the preceding code:

As we can see from the preceding screenshot, the name variable still contains Frankie Kaur as its value, although we have modified it inside the Modify() function. It's because we pass the n variable in the main() function and the Modify() function receives a copy of the value stored in the name variable so that the name variable remains unchanged and contains the original value. We can mutate the n variable if we pass it as the reference, as we can see in the following mutable_2.cpp code:

```
/* mutable_2.cpp */
#include <iostream>

using namespace std;

void Modify(string &name)
{
  name = "Alexis Andrews";
}

auto main() -> int
{
  cout << "[mutable_2.cpp]" << endl;
```

```
    // Initializing a string variable
    string n = "Frankie Kaur";
    cout << "Initial name = " << n;
    cout << endl;

    // Invoking Modify() function
    // to modify the n variable
    Modify(n);

    // Displaying n value
    cout << "After manipulating = " << n;
    cout << endl;

    return 0;
}
```

Just adding the ampersand symbol (&) to the argument of the Modify() function now passes the parameter as a reference. The output on the screen will be like the following screenshot:

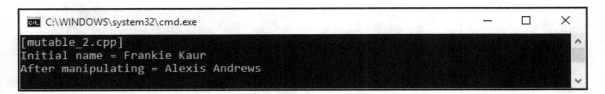

Based on the preceding screenshot, the n variable has now been changed successfully in the Modify() function since we pass by the reference of the n variable, not a value itself. There is also another best approach to mutate the variable using struct or class type, as we can see in the following mutable_2a.cpp code:

```
/* mutable_2a.cpp */
#include <iostream>

using namespace std;

class Name
{
  public:
    string str;
};

void Modify(Name &name)
{
  name.str = "Alexis Andrews";
}
```

```
auto main() -> int
{
  cout << "[mutable_2a.cpp]" << endl;

  // Initializing a string variable
  Name n = {"Frankie Kaur"};
  cout << "Initial name = " << n.str;
  cout << endl;

  // Invoking Modify() function
  // to modify the n variable
  Modify(n);

  // Displaying n value
  cout << "After manipulating = " << n.str;
  cout << endl;

  return 0;
}
```

As we can see in the preceding code, we have a class named `Name` that contains a string variable on it. At the beginning, we instance the `Name` class with an initial value. We then modify the `str` value inside the class. If we run the code, we will get the exact same output comparing with the `mutable_2.cpp` code. However, we see that although the `n` variable didn't change, `name.str` did.

Preventing the modification of a value

The essential point of immutability is preventing value modification. In C++ programming language, there is a keyword to prevent the code modifying a value. The keyword is `const` and we are going to use it in the `const.cpp` code. We have a class named `MyAge` which contains a public field named `age` and we set it as `const`. We will play with this `const` field and the code will look like following:

```
/* const.cpp */
#include <iostream>

using namespace std;

// My Age class will store an age value
class MyAge
{
    public:
      const int age;
```

```
        MyAge(const int initAge = 20) :
         age(initAge)
         {
         }
  };

   auto main() -> int
   {
     cout << "[const.cpp]" << endl;

     // Initializing several MyAge variables
     MyAge AgeNow, AgeLater(8);

     // Displaying age property in AgeNow instance
     cout << "My current age is ";
     cout << AgeNow.age << endl;

     // Displaying age property in AgeLater instance
     cout << "My age in eight years later is ";
     cout << AgeLater.age << endl;

     return 0;
   }
```

As we can see in the preceding code, we instantiate two MyAge class; they are AgeNow and AgeLater. For AgeNow, we use the initial value for age, while, for AgeLater, we give 8 to the age field. The output on the console will be as follow:

However, it's impossible to insert the assignment to age field. The following const_error.cpp code will not be run since the compiler will refuse it:

```
       /* const_error.cpp */
       #include <iostream>

       using namespace std;

       // My Age class will store an age value
       class MyAge
       {
           public:
```

```
      const int age;
      MyAge(const int initAge = 20) :
        age(initAge)
      {
      }
};

auto main() -> int
{
  cout << "[const_error.cpp]" << endl;

  // Initializing several MyAge variables
  MyAge AgeNow, AgeLater(8);

  // Displaying age property in AgeNow instance
  cout << "My current age is ";
  cout << AgeNow.age << endl;

  // Displaying age property in AgeLater instance
  cout << "My age in eight years later is ";
  cout << AgeLater.age << endl;

  // Trying to assign age property
  // in AgeLater instance
  // However, the compiler will refuse it
  AgeLater.age = 10;

  return 0;
}
```

As we can see, we modify the age value to 10. The compiler will refuse to run since the age is set as const and will display the following error:

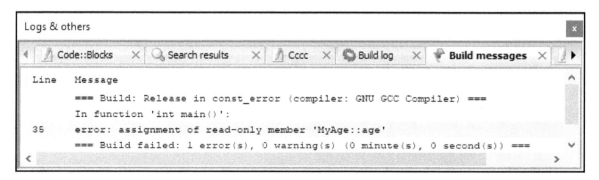

Thus, we have successfully created an immutable object by adding the const keyword.

Applying the first-class function and the pure function to the immutable object

We gained an introduction to the immutable object from the preceding discussion. As you learned in the previous chapter, we can take advantage of the first-class function and pure function to create an immutable programming approach. Let's borrow the code from Chapter 2, *Manipulating Functions in Functional Programming*, that is `first_class_1.cpp`. We will have the `addition()`, `subtraction()`, `multiplication()`, and `division()` methods in our following `first_class_pure_immutable.cpp` code. We will then invoke the pure function on the class and assign the result to the variable. The code is written as follows:

```cpp
/* first_class_pure_immutable.cpp */
#include <iostream>

using namespace std;

// MyValue class stores the value
class MyValue
{
  public:
    const int value;
    MyValue(int v) : value(v)
    {
    }
};

// MyFunction class stores the methods
class MyFunction
{
  public:
    const int x, y;

    MyFunction(int _x, int _y) :
    x(_x), y(_y)
    {
    }

    MyValue addition() const
    {
      return MyValue(x + y);
    }

    MyValue subtraction() const
    {
```

```
        return MyValue(x - y);
    }

  MyValue multiplication() const
  {
      return MyValue(x * y);
  }

  MyValue division() const
  {
      return MyValue(x / y);
  }
};

auto main() -> int
{
  cout << "[first_class_pure_immutable.cpp]" << endl;

  // Setting the initial value
  // for MyFunction class constructor
  int a = 100;
  int b = 10;

  // Displaying initial value
  cout << "Initial value" << endl;
  cout << "a = " << a << endl;
  cout << "b = " << b << endl;
  cout << endl;

  // Constructing the MyFunction class
  MyFunction func(a, b);

  // Generating wrapper for each function
  // in the MyFunction class
  // so it will be the first-class function
  auto callableAdd = mem_fn(&MyFunction::addition);
  auto callableSub = mem_fn(&MyFunction::subtraction);
  auto callableMul = mem_fn(&MyFunction::multiplication);
  auto callableDiv = mem_fn(&MyFunction::division);

  // Invoking the functions
  auto value1 = callableAdd(func);
  auto value2 = callableSub(func);
  auto value3 = callableMul(func);
  auto value4 = callableDiv(func);

  // Displaying result
  cout << "The result" << endl;
```

```
        cout << "addition = " << value1.value << endl;
        cout << "subtraction = " << value2.value << endl;
        cout << "multiplication = " << value3.value << endl;
        cout << "division = " << value4.value << endl;

        return 0;
    }
```

As we can see in the preceding code, the addition(), subtraction(), multiplication(), and division() methods are a pure function as they produce the same output as long as they receive the same input. We also make a class named MyValue and set it as const to make it immutable. Then, to make our function become the first-class function, we wrap each method in the MyFunction class using the mem_fn() function. Afterward, we assign four variables with the function wrapper we've got. The output on the screen should look like the following screenshot:

```
C:\WINDOWS\system32\cmd.exe                              —    □    ×
[first_class_pure_immutable.cpp]
Initial value
a = 100
b = 10

The result
addition = 110
subtraction = 90
multiplication = 1000
division = 10
```

Developing the immutable object

After we discuss the concept of immutability, now let's develop the immutable object. We will start with the mutable object first, then refactor it into an immutable one.

Starting with a mutable object

Now, let's go further. We will create another class to design an immutable object. First, we will create a mutable class named MutableEmployee. We have some fields and methods in that class. The header of the class will be like the following piece of code:

```
/* mutableemployee.h */
#ifndef __MUTABLEEMPLOYEE_H__
#define __MUTABLEEMPLOYEE_H__

#include <string>

class MutableEmployee
{
  private:
    int m_id;
    std::string m_firstName;
    std::string m_lastName;
    double m_salary;

 public:
    MutableEmployee(
      int id,
      const std::string& firstName,
      const std::string& lastName,
      const double& salary);
    MutableEmployee();

    void SetId(const int id);
    void SetFirstName(
     const std::string& FirstName);
    void SetLastName(
     const std::string& LastName);
    void SetSalary(
     const double& Salary);

    int Id() const {return m_id;}
    std::string FirstName() const {return m_firstName;}
    std::string LastName() const {return m_lastName;}
    double Salary() const {return m_salary;}
  };

#endif // End of __MUTABLEEMPLOYEE_H__
```

As we can see, we have four fields--m_id, m_firstName, m_lastName, and m_salary. We also have the definition of four methods to store any value to those fields. The implementation of those methods is as follows:

```cpp
/* mutableemployee.cpp */
#include "mutableemployee.h"

using namespace std;

MutableEmployee::MutableEmployee() :
  m_id(0),
  m_salary(0.0)
{
}

MutableEmployee::MutableEmployee(
  int id,
  const string& firstName,
  const string& lastName,
  const double& salary) :
    m_id(id),
    m_firstName(firstName),
    m_lastName(lastName),
    m_salary(salary)
{
}

void MutableEmployee::SetId(const int id)
{
  m_id = id;
}

void MutableEmployee::SetFirstName(
  const std::string& FirstName) {
    m_firstName = FirstName;
  }

void MutableEmployee::SetLastName(
  const std::string& LastName) {
    m_lastName = LastName;
  }

void MutableEmployee::SetSalary(
  const double& Salary) {
    m_salary = Salary;
  }
```

As we can see in the preceding code, we have a good OOP code in which the members are private; however, we can access them through setters and getters. In other words, any code can change any value so that it is mutable. Now, let's consume the preceding class using this coming `mutable_3.cpp` code. We will instance the class with the initial value and try to mutate them. The code will look as follows:

```cpp
/* mutable_3.cpp */
#include <iostream>
#include "../mutableemployee/mutableemployee.h"

using namespace std;

auto main() -> int
{
  cout << "[mutable_3.cpp]" << endl;

  // Initializing several variables
  string first = "Frankie";
  string last = "Kaur";
  double d = 1500.0;

  // Creating an instance of MutableEmployee
  MutableEmployee me(0, first, last, d);

  // Displaying initial value
  cout << "Content of MutableEmployee instance" << endl;
  cout << "ID : " << me.Id() << endl;
  cout << "Name : " << me.FirstName();
  cout << " " << me.LastName() << endl;
  cout << "Salary : " << me.Salary() << endl << endl;

  // Mutating the instance of MutableEmployee
  me.SetId(1);
  me.SetFirstName("Alexis");
  me.SetLastName("Andrews");
  me.SetSalary(2100.0);

  // Displaying mutate value
  cout << "Content of MutableEmployee after mutating" << endl;
  cout << "ID : " << me.Id() << endl;
  cout << "Name : " << me.FirstName();
  cout << " " << me.LastName() << endl;
  cout << "Salary : " << me.Salary() << endl;

  return 0;
}
```

As we can see in the preceding code, we have the initial value stored in three variables-- `first`, `last`, and `d`. We will then successfully mutate the instance using the setter. The output should be as follows:

```
C:\WINDOWS\system32\cmd.exe                                    —   □   ×
[mutable_3.cpp]
Content of MutableEmployee instance
ID      : 0
Name    : Frankie Kaur
Salary : 1500

Content of MutableEmployee after mutating
ID      : 1
Name    : Alexis Andrews
Salary : 2100
```

The preceding screenshot shows us the mutation result of the `MutableEmployee` class. Since we need to avoid the side effect by avoiding the mutate state, we have to refactor the class to an immutable class.

Refactoring a mutable object into an immutable one

As we discussed earlier, to avoid side effects, we have to design our class to be an immutable object. We will refactor the previous `MutableEmployee` class. Let's take a look at the following header class:

```cpp
/* immutableemployee.h */
#ifndef __IMMUTABLEEMPLOYEE_H__
#define __IMMUTABLEEMPLOYEE_H__

#include <string>

class ImmutableEmployee
{
  private:
    int m_id;
    std::string m_firstName;
    std::string m_lastName;
    double m_salary;
```

```
  public:
    ImmutableEmployee(
      const int id,
      const std::string& firstName,
      const std::string& lastName,
      const double& _salary);
    ImmutableEmployee();

    const int Id() const {
      return m_id;
    }

    const std::string& FirstName() const {
      return m_firstName;
    }

    const std::string& LastName() const {
      return m_lastName;
    }

    const double Salary() const {
     return m_salary;
    }
};

#endif // End of __IMMUTABLEEMPLOYEE_H__
```

As we can see in the preceding header code, we removed the setters from the previous
MutableEmployee class. We did that to make the ImmutableEmployee class immutable.
The implementation of the header can be found in the following code:

```
/* immutableemployee.cpp */
#include "immutableemployee.h"

using namespace std;

ImmutableEmployee::ImmutableEmployee() :
  m_id(0),
  m_salary(0.0)
  {
  }

ImmutableEmployee::ImmutableEmployee(
  const int id,
  const string& firstName,
  const string& lastName,
  const double& salary) :
    m_id(id),
```

```
        m_firstName(firstName),
        m_lastName(lastName),
        m_salary(salary)
   {
   }
```

Now, let's analyze the `ImmutableEmployee` class and compare it with the `MutableEmployee` class. The following is what we should obtain:

- We now set all member variables to `const`, which means the variables can be initialized in the constructor only. This would be the best approach in creating an immutable object. However, the `const` members prevent making a move operation to other members, which is a neat C++11 optimization.
- The getter methods now return the `const` reference instead of the value. Since the immutable object cannot modify the value, it's better to return the reference to them.
- The getters now return the `const` value to avoid the result to be modified by other statements. It also prevents some common errors, like the use of = rather than == in comparison. It declares the fact that we use an immutable type.

The problem occurs if we want to change the `m_firstName` or `m_salary` fields, for instance. To solve this problem, we can add the setter to the `ImmutableEmployee` class. However, it now returns the `ImmutableEmployee` instance instead of mutating the field target. The `immutableemployee.h` code will be as follows:

```cpp
/* immutableemployee.h */
#ifndef __IMMUTABLEEMPLOYEE_H__
#define __IMMUTABLEEMPLOYEE_H__

#include <string>

class ImmutableEmployee
{
  private:
    int m_id;
    std::string m_firstName;
    std::string m_lastName;
    double m_salary;

  public:
    ImmutableEmployee(
       const int id,
       const std::string& firstName,
       const std::string& lastName,
       const double& _salary);
```

```cpp
    ImmutableEmployee();
    ~ImmutableEmployee();

    const int Id() const {
      return m_id;
    }

    const std::string& FirstName() const {
      return m_firstName;
    }

    const std::string& LastName() const {
      return m_lastName;
     }

    const double Salary() const {
      return m_salary;
     }

    const ImmutableEmployee SetId(
      const int id) const {
        return ImmutableEmployee(
          id, m_firstName, m_lastName, m_salary);
      }

  const ImmutableEmployee SetFirstName(
     const std::string& firstName) const {
        return ImmutableEmployee(
          m_id, firstName, m_lastName, m_salary);
      }
  const ImmutableEmployee SetLastName(
     const std::string& lastName) const {
        return ImmutableEmployee(
          m_id, m_firstName, lastName, m_salary);
      }

  const ImmutableEmployee SetSalary(
     const double& salary) const {
        return ImmutableEmployee(
          m_id, m_firstName, m_lastName, salary);
      }
  };

#endif // End of __IMMUTABLEEMPLOYEE_H__
```

As we can see, now, in the `immutableemployee.h` file, we have four setters. They are `SetId`, `SetFirstName`, `SetLastName`, and `SetSalary`. Although the name of setter in the `ImmutableEmployee` class is completely the same as the `MutableEmployee` class, in the `ImmutableEmployee` class, the setters return the instance of the class, as we discussed earlier. By using this `ImmutableEmployee` class, we have to adopt the functional approach since the class is the immutable object. The following code is `immutable_3.cpp`, which we refactor from the `mutable_3.cpp` file:

```cpp
/* immutable_3.cpp */
#include <iostream>
#include "../immutableemployee/immutableemployee.h"

using namespace std;

auto main() -> int
{
  cout << "[immutable_3.cpp]" << endl;

  // Initializing several variables
  string first = "Frankie";
  string last = "Kaur";
  double d = 1500.0;

  // Creating the instance of ImmutableEmployee
  ImmutableEmployee me(0, first, last, d);

  // Displaying initial value
  cout << "Content of ImmutableEmployee instance" << endl;
  cout << "ID : " << me.Id() << endl;
  cout << "Name : " << me.FirstName()
    << " " << me.LastName() << endl;
  cout << "Salary : " << me.Salary() << endl << endl;

  // Modifying the initial value
  ImmutableEmployee me2 = me.SetId(1);
  ImmutableEmployee me3 = me2.SetFirstName("Alexis");
  ImmutableEmployee me4 = me3.SetLastName("Andrews");
  ImmutableEmployee me5 = me4.SetSalary(2100.0);

  // Displaying the new value
  cout << "Content of ImmutableEmployee after modifying" << endl;
  cout << "ID : " << me5.Id() << endl;
  cout << "Name : " << me5.FirstName()
    << " " << me5.LastName() << endl;
  cout << "Salary : " << me5.Salary() << endl;

  return 0;
```

}

As we see in the preceding code, we modify the content by instancing four other
`ImmutableEmployee` classes--me2, me3, me4, and me5. This resembles what we did in
`immutable_1.cpp`. However, we now deal with a class. The output of the preceding code
should look like the following screenshot:

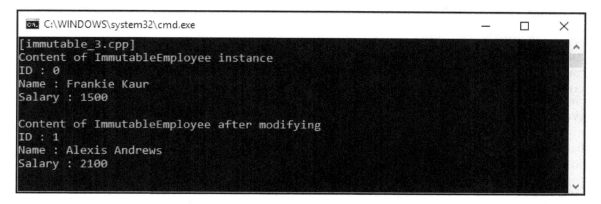

By obtaining the preceding output, we can say that we have successfully modified the
instance of the `ImmutableEmployee` class without mutating it.

Enumerating the benefits of being immutable

After our discussion, we now know that an immutable object is an essential part of the
functional programming. The following are the benefits we can get from the immutable
object:

- We won't deal with the side effect. It's because we have ensured that no outside
  state is modified. We also create a new object every time we intend to change the
  value inside the object.
- There is no invalid object's state. It's because we will always be in an inconsistent
  state. If we forget to invoke a particular method, we will definitely get the correct
  state since there is no connection between methods.
- It will be thread-safe since we can run many methods together with no need to
  lock the first method that is run in the pool. In other words, we will never face
  any synchronization issues.

Summary

First, in this chapter, we tried to modify a local variable in a functional way. We cannot reuse the variable we created; instead, we have to create another one when we need to modify it. We also discussed the technique to modify the variable we passed to another function. Instead of passing the argument by value, we have to pass it by reference to make it change.

Then, we dug the use of the `const` keyword to provide the immutable behavior to the function. By using this keyword, we can ensure that the variable inside the class cannot be modified. Another discussion was about applying the first-class and pure functions--things you learned in the previous chapter--to gain the power of immutability.

We also created the mutable class and then refactored it into an immutable class. We are now able to distinguish the mutable and immutable object and can apply it in our functional code. Lastly, in this chapter, we enumerated the benefit of the immutable object, so we are confident to use it in our daily code.

Another question may appear in our minds now. How do we run the recursion if we have to deal with the immutable object? We cannot even modify a single variable in the method. In the next chapter, we will sort this problem out by discussing recursion in functional programming.

4
Repeating Method Invocation Using Recursive Algorithm

In the last chapter, you learned about immutable states that make us not deal with the side effect. In this chapter, let's take a look at the concept of recursion. As a programmer in object-oriented programming, we usually use iteration to repeat the process instead of recursion. However, recursion gives more benefit than iteration. For instance, some problems (mathematics, especially) are solved easily using recursion, and, fortunately, all algorithms can be defined recursively. That makes it much, much easier to visualize and prove. To get to know more about the recursion, the following topics will be discussed in this chapter:

- Differentiating the iteration and recursion invocation
- Recurring the immutable function
- Finding a better way in recursion using tail recursion
- Enumerating three kinds of recursion--functional, procedural, and backtracking recursion

Repeating the function invocation recursively

As a programmer, especially in object-oriented programming, we usually use the iteration technique to repeat our process. For now, we will discuss the recursion method to repeat our process and use it in the functional approach. Basically, recursion and iteration perform the same task, which is to solve a complicated task piece by piece then combine the results. However, they have a difference. The iteration process emphasizes that we should keep repeating the process until the task is done, whereas recursion emphasizes that need to break the task up into smaller pieces until we can solve the task, then combine the result. We can use the iteration process when we need to run a certain process until the limit is reached or read a stream until it reaches `eof()`. Also, recursion can give the best value when we use it, for instance, on the calculation of a factorial.

Performing the iteration procedure to repeat the process

We will start with the iteration process. As we discussed earlier, the calculation of a factorial will be better if it's designed using the recursion approach. However, it's possible as well to design it with the iteration approach. Here, we will have a `factorial_iteration_do_while.cpp` code that we can use to calculate the factorial. We will have a function named `factorial ()` that passes a single parameter that will calculate the factorial value we pass in the argument. The code should look like this:

```cpp
/* factorial_iteration_do_while.cpp */
#include <iostream>

using namespace std;

// Function containing
// do-while loop iteration

int factorial (int n)
{
  int result = 1;
  int i = 1;

  // Running iteration using do-while loop
  do
    {
      result *= i;
```

```
    }
    while(++i <= n);

    return result;
}

auto main() -> int
{
    cout << "[factorial_iteration_do_while.cpp]" << endl;

    // Invoking factorial() function nine times
    for(int i = 1; i < 10; ++i)
    {
        cout << i << "! = " << factorial(i) << endl;
    }

    return 0;
}
```

As we can see in the preceding code, we depend on the value of n, which we pass to the factorial() function, in determining how many iterations will occur. Every time the iteration performs, the result variable will be multiplied by the counter i. At the end, the result variable will hold the last result by combining the iteration's result value. The output we should get on the screen is as follows:

```
[factorial_iteration_do_while.cpp]
1! = 1
2! = 2
3! = 6
4! = 24
5! = 120
6! = 720
7! = 5040
8! = 40320
9! = 362880
```

Another technique in an iteration is using another iteration procedure. We can refactor the preceding code to use the `for` loop in the `factorial()` function. The following is the `factorial_iteration_for.cpp` code that is refactored from our preceding `factorial_iteration_do_while.cpp` code:

```cpp
/* factorial_iteration_do_while.cpp */
#include <iostream>

using namespace std;

// Function containing
// for loop iteration
int factorial (int n)
{
    int result = 1;

    // Running iteration using for loop
    for(int i = 1; i <= n; ++i)
    {
        result *= i;
    }

    return result;
}

auto main() -> int
{
    cout << "[factorial_iteration_for.cpp]" << endl;

    // Invoking factorial() function nine times
    for(int i = 1; i < 10; ++i)
    {
        cout << i << "! = " << factorial(i) << endl;
    }

    return 0;
}
```

As we can see, we replace the `do-while` loop with the `for` loop. However, the behavior of the program will be exactly the same, since it will also multiply the current result with the `i` counter each time the iteration performs. At the end of this iteration, we will obtain the final result from this multiplication process. The screen should display the following output:

```
[factorial_iteration_for.cpp]
1! = 1
2! = 2
3! = 6
4! = 24
5! = 120
6! = 720
7! = 5040
8! = 40320
9! = 362880
```

Now that we have successfully performed iteration to gain the factorial purpose, either use the do-while or for loop.

It looks too trivial when we try to refactor the do-while loop into the for loop. As we may know, for loops allow us to run through the loop when we know how many times we'd like it to run through the problem, while the do-while loops give us more flexibility in what we put in it and when it will stop, for instance while(i > 0) or use a Boolean value such as while(true). However, based on the preceding example, we now can say that we can switch the for loop or the do-while loop into recursion.

Performing the recursion procedure to repeat the process

We discussed earlier that recursion gives better performance in functional programming. We also developed the factorial() function in the iteration approach. Now, let's refactor our previous code into factorial_recursion.cpp, which will use the recursion approach rather than the iteration one. The code will perform the same task comparing our previous code. However, we will modify the factorial() function to call itself at the end of the function. The code is written as follows:

```
/* factorial_recursion.cpp */
#include <iostream>

using namespace std;

int factorial(int n)
{
```

```
        // Running recursion here
        if (n == 0)
          return 1;
        else
          return n * factorial (n - 1);
    }

    auto main() -> int
    {
        cout << "[factorial_recursion.cpp]" << endl;

        for(int i = 1; i < 10; ++i)
        {
            cout << i << "! = " << factorial(i) << endl;
        }

        return 0;
    }
```

As we can see, the factorial() function in the preceding code calls itself until n is 0. Each time the function calls itself, it decrements the n parameter. The function will return 1 soon after the passed parameter is 0. We will also get the same output compared to our two previous code blocks, as shown in the following screenshot:

```
Command Prompt                                        —    □    ×
[factorial_iteration_for.cpp]
1! = 1
2! = 2
3! = 6
4! = 24
5! = 120
6! = 720
7! = 5040
8! = 40320
9! = 362880
```

Although recursion gives us the simplicity required to easily maintain code, we have to be aware of the parameter we pass to the recursion function. For instance, in the factorial() function in the factorial_recursion.cpp code, if we pass the negative number to the n < 0 function, we will get the infinity loop, and it can crash our device.

Recurring the immutable function

As we discussed in the previous chapter, we need to loop the immutable function recursively. Let's suppose we have the `fibonacci()` function that is immutable. We then need to refactor it to be a recursive function. The `fibonacci_iteration.cpp` code implements the `fibonacci()` function in the iteration way. The code is written as follows:

```cpp
/* fibonacci_iteration.cpp */
#include <iostream>

using namespace std;

// Function for generating
// Fibonacci sequence using iteration
int fibonacci(int n)
{
  if (n == 0)
    return 0;

  int previous = 0;
  int current = 1;

  for (int i = 1; i < n; ++i)
  {
    int next = previous + current;
    previous = current;
    current = next;
  }

  return current;
}

auto main() -> int
{
  cout << "[fibonacci_iteration.cpp]" << endl;

  // Invoking fibonacci() function ten times
  for(int i = 0; i < 10; ++i)
    {
      cout << fibonacci(i) << " ";
    }
  cout << endl;

  return 0;
}
```

As we can see in the preceding code, the `fibonacci()` function is immutable since it will return the same value each time it gets the exact same n input. The output should look like the following screenshot:

If we need to refactor it to be a recursive function, we can use the following `fibonacci_recursion.cpp` code:

```cpp
/* fibonacci_recursion.cpp */
#include <iostream>
using namespace std;

// Function for generating
// Fibonacci sequence using recursion
int fibonacci(int n)
{
  if(n <= 1)
    return n;

  return fibonacci(n-1) + fibonacci(n-2);
}

auto main() -> int
{
  cout << "[fibonacci_recursion.cpp]" << endl;

  // Invoking fibonacci() function ten times
  for(int i = 0; i < 10; ++i)
  {
    cout << fibonacci(i) << " ";
  }
  cout << endl;

  return 0;
}
```

As we can see, the preceding code has the recursion approach since it calls the function itself at the end of the function. Now that we have the recursion `fibonacci()` function, it will give the following output on the console:

Now, compared to the `fibonacci_iteration.cpp` code, the
`fibonacci_recursion.cpp` code shows the exact same output.

Getting closer to tail recursion

A tail recursion happens when the recursive call is executed at the end by the function. It's considered better than the non-tail recursion code we developed previously because the compiler can optimize the code better. Since the recursive call is the last statement that is executed by the function, there is nothing more to do in this function. The result is that the compiler does not need to save the current function's stack frame. Let's see the following `tail_recursion.cpp` code implementing tail recursion:

```cpp
/* tail_recursion.cpp */
#include <iostream>

using namespace std;

void displayNumber(long long n)
{
  // Displaying the current n value
  cout << n << endl;
  // The last executed statement
  // is the recursive call
  displayNumber(n + 1);
}

auto main() -> int
{
  cout << "[tail_recursion.cpp]" << endl;

  // Invoking the displayNumber() function
  // containing tail recursion
  displayNumber(0);

  return 0;
}
```

As we can see in the preceding code, the `displayNumber()` function is a tail recursive call function since it calls itself at the end of the process. Indeed, if we run the preceding `tail_recursion.cpp` code, the program will not end since it will increase the value of n in the `displayNumber()` function. The program may be crashed when the value of n has reached the maximum value of the `long long` data type. However, the program will not have the stack issued (stack overflowed) since the tail recursion doesn't store a value in the stack.

Also, we can refactor the preceding `displayNumber()` function in the `tail_recursion.cpp` code to use the `goto` keyword instead of calling the function over and over. The refactored code can be seen in the following `tail_recursion_goto.cpp` code:

```cpp
/* tail_recursion_goto.cpp */
#include <iostream>

using namespace std;

void displayNumber(long long n)
{
  loop:
    // Displaying the current n value
    cout << n << endl;

    // Update parameters of recursive call
    // and replace recursive call with goto
    n++;
    goto loop;
}

auto main() -> int
{
  cout << "[tail_recursion_goto.cpp]" << endl;

  // Invoking the displayNumber() function
  // containing tail recursion
  displayNumber(0);

  return 0;
}
```

As we can see in the preceding code, we can remove the last call in the displayNumber() function with the goto keyword. This is how the compiler optimizes the tail recursion by performing a tail-call elimination that will replace the last call with the goto keyword. We will also see that no stack is needed in the displayNumber() function.

> Don't forget to compile the code containing a tail recursion with the optimization option provided by the compiler. Since we use GCC, always enable optimization level 2 (-O2) to gain the optimized code. The effect of not compiling with optimizations enabled, is that our two preceding programs (tail_recursion.cpp and tail_recursion_goto.cpp) will crash with the stack overflowed issue. For more information about the optimizations option in GCC, check out https://gcc.gnu.org/onlinedo cs/gcc-7.1.0/gcc/Optimize-Options.html.

Now, let's create a useful tail recursion call. In the previous section, we have successfully refactored our iteration function into a recursive one. The factorial() function now has become a recursive function and calls itself at the end of the function. However, it is not tail recursion, although the function calls itself at the end of the function. If we look closer, the value returned by factorial(n-1) is used in factorial(n), so the call to factorial(n-1) is not the last thing done by factorial(n).

We can create our factorial_recursion.cpp code to become the tail recursion function. We will develop the following factorial_recursion_tail.cpp code, modify the factorial() function, and add a new function named factorialTail(). The code is written as follows:

```cpp
/* factorial_recursion_tail.cpp */
#include <iostream>

using namespace std;

// Function for calculating factorial
// tail recursion
int factorialTail(int n, int i)
{
  if (n == 0)
    return i;

  return factorialTail(n - 1, n * i);
}

// The caller of tail recursion function
int factorial(int n)
{
```

```
      return factorialTail(n, 1);
}

auto main() -> int
{
    cout << "[factorial_recursion_tail.cpp]" << endl;
    // Invoking fibonacci() function ten times
    for(int i = 1; i < 10; ++i)
    {
        cout << i << "! = " << factorial(i) << endl;
    }

    return 0;
}
```

As we can see, we have moved the factorial() function in the
factorial_recursion.cpp code to the factorialTail() function that requires two
arguments in the factorial_recursion_tail.cpp code. As the result, after we invoke
factorial(i), it will then invoke the factorialTail() function. At the end of this
function, the factorialTail() function is the only function that is invoked. The following
image is the output of the factorial_recursion_tail.cpp code, which is exactly the
same as the factorial_recursion.cpp code. It also proves that we have successfully
refactored the factorial_recursion.cpp code into tail recursion.

```
[factorial_recursion_tail.cpp]
1! = 1
2! = 2
3! = 6
4! = 24
5! = 120
6! = 720
7! = 5040
8! = 40320
9! = 362880
```

Getting acquainted with functional, procedural, and backtracking recursion

So now that we have understood a little about recursion, the recursion function will call itself from inside its body. The recursion will be stopped only when it has reached a certain value. There are three types of recursion that we will discuss right away--**functional recursion**, **procedural recursion**, and **backtracking recursion**; however, these three types of recursion may not be standard terms. Functional recursion is a recursion process that returns some value. Procedural recursion is a recursion process that doesn't return a value, yet performs the action in each recursion it takes. Backtracking recursion is a recursion process to break down the task into a small set of subtasks that can be cancelled if they don't work. Let's consider these recursion types in the following discussion.

Expecting results from functional recursion

In functional recursion, the process tries to solve the problem by combining the results from the subproblems recursively. The result we combine comes from the return value of subproblems. Let's suppose we have a problem to calculate a number to a power, for instance, 2 power 2 is 4 ($2^2 = 4$). By using iteration, we can build a code like the following `exponential_iteration.cpp` code. We have a function named `power()` that will be passed by two arguments--`base` and `exp`. The notation will be $base^{exp}$ and the code looks like this:

```
/* exponential_iteration.cpp */
#include <iostream>

using namespace std;

// Calculating the power of number
// using iteration
int power(int base, int exp)
{
  int result = 1;

  for(int i = 0; i < exp; ++i)
    {
      result *= base;
    }

  return(result);
}
```

```
auto main() -> int
{
  cout << "[exponential_iteration.cpp]" << endl;

  // Invoking power() function six times
  for(int i = 0; i <= 5; ++i)
  {
    cout << "power (2, " << i << ") = ";
    cout << power(2, i) << endl;
  }

  return 0;
}
```

As we can see in the preceding code, we use the iteration version first, before we go to the recursive one, since we usually use the iteration most on a daily basis. We combine the `result` value in each iteration by multiplying it by the `base` value. If we run the preceding code, we will get the following output on the console:

Now, let's refactor our preceding code to the recursive version. We will have the `exponential_recursion.cpp` code that will have the same `power()` function signature. However, we will not use the `for` loop instead of the recursion that the function calls itself at the end of the function. The code should be written as follows:

```
/* exponential_recursion.cpp */
#include <iostream>

using namespace std;

// Calculating the power of number
// using recursion
int power(int base, int exp)
{
  if(exp == 0)
    return 1;
```

```
      else
        return base * power(base, exp - 1);
    }

    auto main() -> int
    {
      cout << "[exponential_recursion.cpp]" << endl;

      // Invoking power() function six times
      for(int i = 0; i <= 5; ++i)
      {
        cout << "power (2, " << i << ") = ";
        cout << power(2, i) << endl;
      }

      return 0;
    }
```

As we discussed earlier that functional recursion returns value, the power() function is a functional recursion since it returns the int value. We will get the final result from the value returned by each subfunction. As a result, we will get the following output on the console:

```
Command Prompt                                              —    □    ×
[exponential_recursion.cpp]
power (2, 0) = 1
power (2, 1) = 2
power (2, 2) = 4
power (2, 3) = 8
power (2, 4) = 16
power (2, 5) = 32
```

Running a task recursively in procedural recursion

So, we have a functional recursion that expects the return value from the function. Sometimes, we don't need the return value since we run the task from inside the function. To achieve that purpose, we can use procedural recursion. Let's suppose we want to permute a short string to find all possible arrangements of it. Instead of returning the value, we just need to print the result every time the recursion is performed.

We have the following `permutation.cpp` code to demonstrate this task. It has the `permute()` function that will be invoked once, then it will invoke the `doPermute()` function recursively. The code should be written as follows:

```cpp
/* permutation.cpp */
#include <iostream>

using namespace std;

// Calculation the permutation
// of the given string
void doPermute(
  const string &chosen,
  const string &remaining)
  {
   if(remaining == "")
   {
      cout << chosen << endl;
   }
   else
   {
     for(uint32_t u = 0; u < remaining.length(); ++u)
     {
        doPermute(
          chosen + remaining[u],
          remaining.substr(0, u)
          + remaining.substr(u + 1));
     }
   }
}

// The caller of doPermute() function
void permute(
  const string &s)
{
  doPermute("", s);
}

auto main() -> int
{
  cout << "[permutation.cpp]" << endl;

  // Initializing str variable
  // then ask user to fill in
  string str;
  cout << "Permutation of a string" << endl;
  cout << "Enter a string: ";
  getline(cin, str);
```

```
// Finding the possibility of the permutation
// by calling permute() function
cout << endl << "The possibility permutation of ";
cout << str << endl;
permute(str);

return 0;
}
```

As we can see in the preceding code, we ask the user to input a string, then the code will find the possibility of this permutation using the `permute()` function. It will start with the empty string in `doPermute()` since the given string from the user is possible also. The output on the console should be as follows:

```
[permutation.cpp]
Permutation of a string
Enter a string: xyz

The possibility permutation of xyz
xyz
xzy
yxz
yzx
zxy
zyx
```

Backtracking recursion

As we discussed earlier, we can undo the process if the subtask doesn't work. Let's try with a labyrinth where we have to find the way from the starting point to the finishing point. Let's suppose we have to find the way from S to F as in the following labyrinth:

```
# # # # # # # #
# S           #
# # #   # # # #
#   #   # # # #
#             #
#   # # # # # #
#           F #
# # # # # # # #
```

To solve this problem, we have to decide the route we need, to find the finishing point. However, we will assume that each choice is good until we prove it's not. The recursion will return a Boolean value to mark whether it's the right way or not. If we choose the wrong way, the call stack unwinds and it will undo the choice. First, we will draw the labyrinth in our code. In the following code, there will be the createLabyrinth() and displayLabyrinth() functions. The code looks like this:

```cpp
/* labyrinth.cpp */
#include <iostream>
#include <vector>

using namespace std;

vector<vector<char>> createLabyrinth()
{
  // Initializing the multidimensional vector
  // labyrinth
  // # is a wall
  // S is the starting point
  // E is the finishing point
  vector<vector<char>> labyrinth =
  {
    {'#', '#', '#', '#', '#', '#', '#', '#'},
    {'#', 'S', ' ', ' ', ' ', ' ', ' ', '#'},
    {'#', '#', '#', ' ', '#', '#', '#', '#'},
    {'#', ' ', '#', ' ', '#', '#', '#', '#'},
    {'#', ' ', ' ', ' ', ' ', ' ', ' ', '#'},
    {'#', ' ', '#', '#', '#', '#', '#', '#'},
    {'#', ' ', ' ', ' ', ' ', ' ', 'F', '#'},
    {'#', '#', '#', '#', '#', '#', '#', '#'}
  };

  return labyrinth;
}

void displayLabyrinth(vector<vector<char>> labyrinth)
{
  cout << endl;
  cout << "====================" << endl;
  cout << "The Labyrinth" << endl;
  cout << "====================" << endl;

  // Displaying all characters in labyrinth vector
  for (int i = 0; i < rows; i++)
  {
    for (int j = 0; j < cols; j++)
    {
```

```
            cout << labyrinth[i][j] << " ";
        }
        cout << endl;
    }
    cout << "====================" << endl << endl;
}

auto main() -> int
{
    vector<vector<char>> labyrinth = createLabyrinth();
    displayLabyrinth(labyrinth);

    string line;
    cout << endl << "Press enter to continue..." << endl;
    getline(cin, line);

    return 0;
}
```

As we can see, there's no recursion in the preceding code. The createLabyrinth()
function just creates a two-dimensional array that contains the pattern of the labyrinth,
whereas displayLabyrinth() just shows the array to console. We will see the following
output on the console if we run the preceding code:

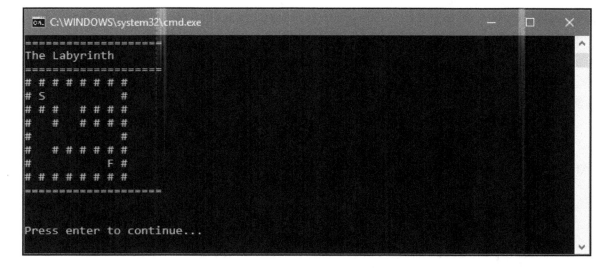

From the preceding screenshot, we can see there are two points there--S is the starting point and F is the finishing point. The code has to find the way to reach F from S. The expected route should be as follows:

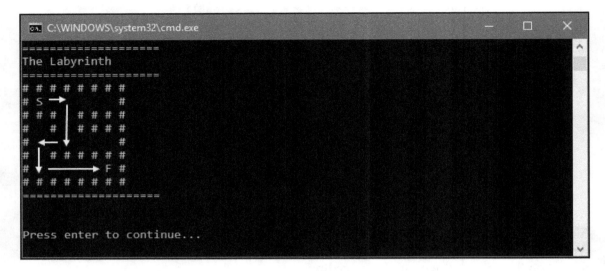

The white arrow on the preceding screenshot is a path we expected to reach F from S. Now, let's develop the code to solve this labyrinth problem. We will create a function named navigate to find the possible route by figuring out these three states:

- If we find F in the [x,y] position, for instance labyrinth[2][4], we have solved the problem then just return true as the return value.
- If the [x,y] position is #, it means that we face the wall and have to revisit the other [x,y] position.
- Otherwise, we print * on that position to mark that we have visited it.

After we have analyzed the three states, we will start with the recursive cases as follows:

- The path seeker will go upward if it can navigate to row – 1, and it's greater than or equal to 0 (row – 1 >= 0 && navigate(labyrinth, row – 1, col))
- The path seeker will go downward if it can navigate to row + 1, and it's smaller than 8 (row + 1 < 8 && navigate(labyrinth, row + 1, col))
- The path seeker will go to the left if it can navigate to col – 1, and it's greater than or equal to 0 (col – 1 >= 0 && navigate(labyrinth, row, col – 1))

- The path seeker will go to the right if it can navigate to `col + 1`, and it's smaller than 8 (`col + 1 < 8 && navigate(labyrinth, row, col + 1)`)

We will have the `navigate()` function as follows:

```
bool navigate(
  vector<vector<char>> labyrinth,
  int row,
  int col)
{
  // Displaying labyrinth
  displayLabyrinth(labyrinth);

  cout << "Checking cell (";
  cout << row << "," << col << ")" << endl;

  // Pause 1 millisecond
  // before navigating
  sleep(1);

  if (labyrinth[row][col] == 'F')
  {
    cout << "Yeayy.. ";
    cout << "Found the finish flag ";
    cout << "at point (" << row << ",";
    cout << col << ")" << endl;
    return (true);
  }
  else if (
    labyrinth[row][col] == '#' ||
    labyrinth[row][col] == '*')
  {
    return (false);
  }
  else if (labyrinth[row][col] == ' ')
  {
    labyrinth[row][col] = '*';
  }
  if ((row + 1 < rows) &&
    navigate(labyrinth, row + 1, col))
    return (true);

  if ((col + 1 < cols) &&
    navigate(labyrinth, row, col + 1))
    return (true);

  if ((row - 1 >= 0) &&
```

```
        navigate(labyrinth, row - 1, col))
        return (true);

    if ((col - 1 >= 0) &&
        navigate(labyrinth, row, col - 1))
        return (true);

    return (false);
}
```

We now have the `navigate()` function to find out the correct path to find F. However, before we run the `navigate()` function, we have to ensure that S is there. We then have to develop the helper function named `isLabyrinthSolvable()`. It will loop through the labyrinth array and will inform whether S is there or not. The following code snippet is the implementation of the `isLabyrinthSolvable()` function:

```
bool isLabyrinthSolvable(
    vector<vector<char>> labyrinth)
{
    int start_row = -1;
    int start_col = -1;
    for (int i = 0; i < rows; i++)
    {
        for (int j = 0; j < cols; j++)
        {
            if (labyrinth[i][j] == 'S')
            {
                start_row = i;
                start_col = j;
                break;
            }
        }
    }

    if (start_row == -1 || start_col == -1)
    {
        cout << "No valid starting point found!" << endl;
        return (false);
    }

    cout << "Starting at point (" << start_row << ",";
    cout << start_col << ")" << endl;

    return navigate(labyrinth, start_row, start_col);
}
```

As we can see in the preceding code snippet, we mention the `rows` and `cols` variables. We will initialize them as global variables, as we can see in the following code snippet:

```cpp
const int rows = 8;
const int cols = 8;
```

Now, let's take a look at the following code if we insert the `navigate()` and `isLabyrinthSolvable()` functions to the `labyrinth.cpp` code:

```cpp
/* labyrinth.cpp */
#include <iostream>
#include <vector>
#include <unistd.h>

using namespace std;

const int rows = 8;
const int cols = 8;

vector<vector<char>> createLabyrinth()
{
  // Initializing the multidimensional vector
  // labyrinth
  // # is a wall
  // S is the starting point
  // E is the finishing point
  vector<vector<char>> labyrinth =
  {
    {'#', '#', '#', '#', '#', '#', '#', '#'},
    {'#', 'S', ' ', ' ', ' ', ' ', ' ', '#'},
    {'#', '#', '#', ' ', '#', '#', '#', '#'},
    {'#', ' ', '#', ' ', '#', '#', '#', '#'},
    {'#', ' ', ' ', ' ', ' ', ' ', ' ', '#'},
    {'#', ' ', '#', '#', '#', '#', '#', '#'},
    {'#', ' ', ' ', ' ', ' ', ' ', 'F', '#'},
    {'#', '#', '#', '#', '#', '#', '#', '#'}
  };

  return labyrinth;
}

void displayLabyrinth(
  vector<vector<char>> labyrinth)
{
  cout << endl;
  cout << "====================" << endl;
  cout << "The Labyrinth" << endl;
  cout << "====================" << endl;
```

```cpp
    // Displaying all characters in labyrinth vector
    for (int i = 0; i < rows; i++)
    {
      for (int j = 0; j < cols; j++)
      {
          cout << labyrinth[i][j] << " ";
      }
      cout << endl;
    }
  cout << "====================" << endl << endl;
}

bool navigate(
  vector<vector<char>> labyrinth,
  int row,
  int col)
{
  // Displaying labyrinth
  displayLabyrinth(labyrinth);

  cout << "Checking cell (";
  cout << row << "," << col << ")" << endl;

  // Pause 1 millisecond
  // before navigating
  sleep(1);

  if (labyrinth[row][col] == 'F')
  {
    cout << "Yeayy.. ";
    cout << "Found the finish flag ";
    cout << "at point (" << row << ",";
    cout << col << ")" << endl;
    return (true);
  }
  else if (
    labyrinth[row][col] == '#' ||
    labyrinth[row][col] == '*')
   {
     return (false);
   }
  else if (labyrinth[row][col] == ' ')
  {
    labyrinth[row][col] = '*';
  }

  if ((row + 1 < rows) &&
    navigate(labyrinth, row + 1, col))
```

```
    return (true);

  if ((col + 1 < cols) &&
    navigate(labyrinth, row, col + 1))
    return (true);

  if ((row - 1 >= 0) &&
    navigate(labyrinth, row - 1, col))
    return (true);

  if ((col - 1 >= 0) &&
    navigate(labyrinth, row, col - 1))
    return (true);

    return (false);
}

bool isLabyrinthSolvable(
  vector<vector<char>> labyrinth)
{
 int start_row = -1;
 int start_col = -1;
 for (int i = 0; i < rows; i++)
 {
    for (int j = 0; j < cols; j++)
    {
        if (labyrinth[i][j] == 'S')
        {
            start_row = i;
            start_col = j;
            break;
        }
    }
 }

 if (start_row == -1 || start_col == -1)
 {
    cerr << "No valid starting point found!" << endl;
    return (false);
 }

 cout << "Starting at point (" << start_row << ",";
 cout << start_col << ")" << endl;

 return navigate(labyrinth, start_row, start_col);
}

auto main() -> int
```

```
    {
        vector<vector<char>> labyrinth = createLabyrinth();
        displayLabyrinth(labyrinth);

        string line;
        cout << endl << "Press enter to continue..." << endl;
        getline(cin, line);

        if (isLabyrinthSolvable(labyrinth))
            cout << "Labyrinth solved!" << endl;
        else
            cout << "Labyrinth could not be solved!" << endl;

        return 0;
    }
```

As we can see in the preceding quote, in the `main()` function, we first run the `isLabyrinthSolvable()` function, which, in turn, invokes the `navigate()` function. The `navigate()` function will then go through the labyrinth to find out the correct path. The following is the output of the code:

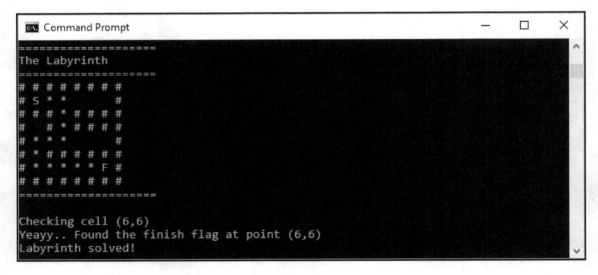

However, if we trace how the program solves the labyrinth, it faces the wrong route when it finds the finish flag, as we can see in the following screenshot:

As we can see, there is a white square in the preceding screenshot. It's the wrong choice when it is looking for the correct path. Once it meets an obstacle, it goes back and finds the other ways. It will also undo the choice it has made. Let's see the following screenshot that shows us when the recursion finds another route and undoes the previous choice:

In the preceding screenshot, we can see that the recursion tries another route and the previously failed route has disappeared since the backtrack recursion undoes the route. The recursion now has the correct path, and it can just continue until it finds the finish flag. As a result, we now have successfully developed the backtracking recursion.

Summary

This chapter has given us the technique for repeating the function invocation by using iteration and recursion. However, since recursion is more functional than iteration, we emphasized our discussion on recursion instead of iteration. We started with the difference between iteration and recursion. We then continued the discussion about refactoring the immutable function to become a recursive immutable function.

After we learned about the recursion, we found other better recursion techniques. We also discussed tail recursion to get this improved technique. Lastly, we enumerated three kinds of recursion--functional, procedural, and backtracking recursion. We usually use functional recursion when we expect the return value for the recursion. Otherwise, we use procedural recursion. And, if we need to break down the problem and undo the recursion performance when it doesn't work, we can use backtracking recursion to solve the problem.

In the next chapter, we will discuss lazy evaluation to make the code run faster. This will make the code become efficient since it will make sure that unnecessary code won't be executed.

5
Procrastinating the Execution Process Using Lazy Evaluation

In the previous chapter, we discussed recursion for repeating the function invocation in the functional approach. Now, we will discuss lazy evaluation that can make our code become more efficient since it will only run when we need it. We will also apply recursion, the topic we talked about in the previous chapter, to produce the lazy code.

In this chapter, we discuss **lazy evaluation** to make code run faster. This will make the code become efficient since it will make sure that unnecessary code won't be executed. The following are the topics we will discuss to dive into lazy evaluation:

- Distinguishing the difference between eager and lazy evaluation
- Optimizing code using the caching technique
- Refactoring eager evaluation into lazy evaluation
- Designing the useful classes that can be reused in others' functional code

Evaluating the expression

Every programming language has its own strategy to determine when to evaluate the arguments of a function call and what type of value that has to be passed to the parameter. There are two kinds of strategy evaluation that are mostly used in a programming language--**strict** (eager) evaluation and **non-strict** (lazy) evaluation.

Running the expression immediately with strict evaluation

Strict evaluation is used in the most imperative programming language. It will immediately execute the code we have. Let's suppose we have the following equation:

```
int i = (x + (y * z));
```

In a strict evaluation, the innermost bracket will be calculated first, then work outwards for the preceding equation. This means we will calculate $y * z$, then add the result to x. To make it clearer, let's see the following `strict.cpp` code:

```cpp
/* strict.cpp */
#include <iostream>

using namespace std;

int OuterFormula(int x, int yz)
{
  // For logging purpose only
  cout << "Calculate " << x << " + ";
  cout << "InnerFormula(" << yz << ")";
  cout << endl;

  // Returning the calculation result
  return x * yz;
}

int InnerFormula(int y, int z)
{
  // For logging purpose only
  cout << "Calculate " << y << " * ";
  cout << z << endl;
  // Returning the calculation result
  return y * z;
}

auto main() -> int
{
  cout << "[strict.cpp]" << endl;

  // Initializing three int variables
  // for the calculation
  int x = 4;
  int y = 3;
  int z = 2;
```

```
    // Calculating the expression
    cout << "Calculate " << x <<" + ";
    cout << "(" << y << " * " << z << ")";
    cout << endl;
    int result = OuterFormula(x, InnerFormula(y, z));

    // For logging purpose only
    cout << x << " + ";
    cout << "(" << y << " * " << z << ")";
    cout << " = " << result << endl;
    return 0;
}
```

As we discussed earlier, the execution of the preceding code will be y * z first, then we will add the result to x, as we can see in the following output:

```
Command Prompt                                         —    □    ×
[strict.cpp]
Calculate 4 + (3 * 2)
Calculate 3 * 2
Calculate 4 + InnerFormula(6)
4 + (3 * 2) = 24
```

The preceding execution order is what we usually expect. However, in non-strict evaluation, we will reorder this execution process.

Delaying the expression with non-strict evaluation

In a non-strict evaluation, the + operator is reduced first, and then we reduce the inner formula, which is (y * z). We will see that the evaluation will be started from the outside to the inside. We will refactor our previous strict.cpp code to make it become a non-strict evaluation. The code should be like the following non_strict.cpp code:

```
/* non_strict.cpp */
#include <functional>
#include <iostream>

using namespace std;

int OuterFormulaNonStrict(
  int x,
```

```cpp
    int y,
    int z,
    function<int(int, int)> yzFunc)
    {
       // For logging purpose only
       cout << "Calculate " << x << " + ";
       cout << "InnerFormula(" << y << ", ";
       cout << z << ")" << endl;

       // Returning the calculation result
       return x * yzFunc(y, z);
    }

int InnerFormula(int y, int z)
{
  // For logging purpose only
  cout << "Calculate " << y << " * ";
  cout << z << endl;

  // Returning the calculation result
  return y * z;
}

auto main() -> int
{
  cout << "[non_strict.cpp]" << endl;

  // Initializing three int variables
  // for the calculation
  int x = 4;
  int y = 3;
  int z = 2;

  // Calculating the expression
  cout << "Calculate " << x <<" + ";
  cout << "(" << y << " * " << z << ")";
  cout << endl;
  int result = OuterFormulaNonStrict(x, y, z, InnerFormula);

  // For logging purpose only
  cout << x << " + ";
  cout << "(" << y << " * " << z << ")";
  cout << " = " << result << endl;

  return 0;
}
```

As we can see, we modify the `OuterFormula()` function in the `strict.cpp` code into an `OuterFormulaNonStrict()` function in the `non_strict.cpp` code. In the `OuterFormulaNonStrict()` function, we pass a function as the argument in addition to the three variables--x, y, and z. As a result, the order of execution of the preceding expression is changed. Here is what we should see on the console screen when we run the `non_strict.cpp` code:

```
[non_strict.cpp]
Calculate 4 + (3 * 2)
Calculate 4 + InnerFormula(3, 2)
Calculate 3 * 2
4 + (3 * 2) = 24
```

From the preceding output, we have proved that our code is performing non-strict evaluation since it now calculates the addition operator (+) first instead of the multiplication (*). However, the result is still correct, although the order has been changed.

The basic concept of lazy evaluation

Before we create a lazy code, let's discuss the basic concepts of lazy evaluation. We will use the delaying process to make our code lazy, the caching technique to increase the performance of the code by avoiding needless calculations, and the optimizing technique to speed up the code by storing the results of expensive function calls and returning the cached result when the same inputs occur again. After we have looked at these techniques, we will try to develop the real lazy code.

Delaying the process

The basic concept of laziness is delaying a process. In this section, we will discuss how to delay the execution of a particular process. We will create a new class named `Delay`. We will pass a function into it when we construct the class. The function won't be run unless we invoke the `Fetch()` method. The implementation of the function is as follows:

```
template<class T> class Delay
{
  private:
    function<T()> m_func;
```

```
public:
  Delay(
    function<T()> func)
    : m_func(func)
    {
    }

  T Fetch()
  {
    return m_func();
  }
};
```

Now, let's consume the `Delay` class to procrastinate the execution. We will create a file named `delaying.cpp` that will run two functions--`multiply` and `division`. However, these two functions will only be run after we call the `Fetch()` method. The content of the file is as follows:

```cpp
/* delaying.cpp */
#include <iostream>
#include <functional>

using namespace std;

template<class T> class Delay
{
  private:
    function<T()> m_func;

  public:
    Delay(function<T()> func) : m_func(func)
    {
    }

    T Fetch()
    {
      return m_func();
    }
};

auto main() -> int
{
  cout << "[delaying.cpp]" << endl;

  // Initializing several int variables
  int a = 10;
  int b = 5;
```

```
  cout << "Constructing Delay<> named multiply";
  cout << endl;
  Delay<int> multiply([a, b]()
  {
    cout << "Delay<> named multiply";
    cout << " is constructed." << endl;
    return a * b;
  });

  cout << "Constructing Delay<> named division";
  cout << endl;
  Delay<int> division([a, b]()
  {
    cout << "Delay<> named division ";
    cout << "is constructed." << endl;
    return a / b;
  });

  cout << "Invoking Fetch() method in ";
  cout << "multiply instance." << endl;
  int c = multiply.Fetch();

  cout << "Invoking Fetch() method in ";
  cout << "division instance." << endl;
  int d = division.Fetch();

  // Displaying the result
  cout << "The result of a * b = " << c << endl;
  cout << "The result of a / b = " << d << endl;

  return 0;
}
```

As we discussed in `Chapter 1`, *Diving into Modern C++*, we can use a Lambda expression to build the `multiply` and `division` functions. We then pass them in each `Delay` constructor. In this stage, the function is not run yet. It will be run after the `Fetch()` method is invoked--`multiply.Fetch()` and `division.Fetch()`. The output we will see on the screen should look like the following screenshot:

```
[delaying.cpp]
Constructing Delay<> named multiply
Constructing Delay<> named division
Invoking Fetch() method in multiply instance.
Delay<> named multiply is constructed. ◄────────
Invoking Fetch() method in division instance.
Delay<> named division is constructed. ◄────────
The result of a * b = 50
The result of a / b = 2
```

As we can see in the preceding output screenshot, the `multiply` and `division` instance is constructed when the `Fetch()` method is invoked (see the two white arrows), not when the constructor of the `Delay` class is invoked. Now, we have successfully delayed the execution, and we can say that the process is only executed when it is needed.

Caching the value using the memoization technique

We now have successfully delayed the execution of the function by consuming the `Delay` class. However, since the function of the `Delay` class instance will be run each time the `Fetch()` method is invoked, an unexpected result might occur if the function is not pure or has side effects. Let's refactor our previous `delaying.cpp` code by modifying the `multiply` function. This function now becomes a non-pure function since it depends on an outside variable. The code should look like this:

```cpp
/* delaying_non_pure.cpp */
#include <iostream>
#include <functional>

using namespace std;

template<class T> class Delay
{
```

```cpp
  private:
    function<T()> m_func;

  public:
    Delay(function<T()> func) : m_func(func)
    {
    }

    T Fetch()
    {
      return m_func();
    }
};

auto main() -> int
{
  cout << "[delaying_non_pure.cpp]" << endl;

  // Initializing several int variables
  int a = 10;
  int b = 5;
  int multiplexer = 0;

  // Constructing Delay<> named multiply_impure
  Delay<int> multiply_impure([&]()
  {
    return multiplexer * a * b;
  });

  // Invoking Fetch() method in multiply_impure instance
  // multiple times
  for (int i = 0; i < 5; ++i)
  {
    ++multiplexer;
    cout << "Multiplexer = " << multiplexer << endl;
    cout << "a * b = " << multiply_impure.Fetch();
    cout << endl;
  }

  return 0;
}
```

As we can see in the preceding code, we now have a new Lambda expression named `multiply_impure`, which is the refactored version of the `multiply` function we created in the `delaying.cpp` code. The `multiply_impure` function depends on the `multiplexer` variable, whose value will be increased each time before we invoke the `Fetch()` method. The following is the screenshot output we should see on the screen:

```
[delaying_non_pure.cpp]
Multiplexer = 1
a * b = 50
Multiplexer = 2
a * b = 100
Multiplexer = 3
a * b = 150
Multiplexer = 4
a * b = 200
Multiplexer = 5
a * b = 250
```

As we can see, the `Fetch()` method gives a different result each time it's invoked. We now have to refactor the `Delay` class to ensure that it will return the exact same result each time the `Fetch()` method runs the function with the same passed arguments. To achieve it, we will use the memoization technique that stores the results of the function calls and returns the cached result when the same inputs occur again.

We will rename the `Delay` class to `Memoization` class. This will not only delay the function call, it will also record the function with specific passed arguments. So the next time the function with those arguments occurs, the function itself will not be run but it will just return the cached result instead. To ease our discussion, let's take a look at the following `Memoization` class implementation:

```
template<class T> class Memoization
{
  private:
    T const & (*m_subRoutine)(Memoization *);
    mutable T m_recordedFunc;
    function<T()> m_func;

    static T const & ForceSubroutine(Memoization * d)
    {
      return d->DoRecording();
    }
```

```
    static T const & FetchSubroutine(Memoization * d)
    {
      return d->FetchRecording();
    }

    T const & FetchRecording()
    {
      return m_recordedFunc;
    }

    T const & DoRecording()
    {
      m_recordedFunc = m_func();
      m_subRoutine = &FetchSubroutine;
      return FetchRecording();
    }

  public:
    Memoization(function<T()> func) : m_func(func),
     m_subRoutine(&ForceSubroutine),
     m_recordedFunc(T())
    {
    }

    T Fetch()
    {
      return m_subRoutine(this);
    }
};
```

As we can see in the preceding code snippet, we now have FetchRecording() and DoRecording() to get and set the function we have stored. Moreover, when the class is constructed, it will record the passed function and save it to m_subRoutine. The class will inspect m_subRoutine when the Fetch() method is called and find whether it has the value from the function with current passed arguments. If yes, it simply returns the value from m_subRoutine instead of running the function. Now, let's see the following delaying_non_pure_memoization.cpp code, that consumes the Memoization class:

```
/* delaying_non_pure_memoization.cpp */
#include <iostream>
#include <functional>

using namespace std;

template<class T> class Memoization
{
  private:
```

```cpp
    T const & (*m_subRoutine)(Memoization *);
    mutable T m_recordedFunc;
    function<T()> m_func;

    static T const & ForceSubroutine(Memoization * d)
    {
      return d->DoRecording();
    }
    static T const & FetchSubroutine(Memoization * d)
    {
      return d->FetchRecording();
    }

    T const & FetchRecording()
    {
      return m_recordedFunc;
    }

    T const & DoRecording()
    {
      m_recordedFunc = m_func();
      m_subRoutine = &FetchSubroutine;
      return FetchRecording();
    }

  public:
    Memoization(function<T()> func) : m_func(func),
      m_subRoutine(&ForceSubroutine),
      m_recordedFunc(T())
    {
    }

    T Fetch()
    {
      return m_subRoutine(this);
    }
};

auto main() -> int
{
  cout << "[delaying_non_pure_memoization.cpp]" << endl;

  // Initializing several int variables
  int a = 10;
  int b = 5;
  int multiplexer = 0;

  // Constructing Memoization<> named multiply_impure
```

```
Memoization<int> multiply_impure([&]()
{
  return multiplexer * a * b;
});

// Invoking Fetch() method in multiply_impure instance
// multiple times
for (int i = 0; i < 5; ++i)
{
  ++multiplexer;
  cout << "Multiplexer = " << multiplexer << endl;
  cout << "a * b = " << multiply_impure.Fetch();
  cout << endl;
}

return 0;
}
```

From the preceding code snippet, we see we don't have much modification in the main()
function. What we modify is only the class type we use for the multiply_impure variable,
from Delay to Memoization. However, the result has now changed since we will get the
exact same return value from the five times invocation of the multiply_impure()
function. Let's take a look at the following screenshot to prove it:

From the preceding screenshot, we can see that even the value of the Multiplexer is
increased and the return of the calculation is always the same. This is because the return
value of the first function invocation is recorded, so there's no need to run the function
again for the remaining invocation.

As we discussed in Chapter 2, *Manipulating Functions in Functional Programming*, having an impure function seems wrong in functional programming. Hiding an impure function behind memoization might also cause a bug if the code really needs a different result (non-cached result). Use the preceding technique for caching the impure function wisely.

Optimizing the code using the memoization technique

Memoization is quite useful for applying in a non-pure function or a function that has been the side effect. However, it can also be used to optimize the code. By using memoization, the code we have developed will be run faster. Let's suppose we need to run the exact same functions with the exact same passed arguments multiple times. It will be faster if the code fetches the value from the place we record the value instead of running the function. It would also be better for an expensive function call because by using memoization, we don't need to execute the unnecessary expensive function call over and over again.

Let's create a code to discuss the further optimization. We will use the Delay class to demonstrate it's not an optimized code compared to the Memoization class. We will have the not_optimize_code.cpp code that will consume the Delay class. In this unoptimized code, we will call the fibonacci() function that we created in Chapter 4, *Repeating Method Invocation Using Recursive Algorithm*. We will pass 40 as the argument to the fibonacci() function and call the Fetch() method from the fib40 class instance five times. We will also calculate the elapsed time in each invocation of the method, using the high_resolution_clock class resided in the chrono header, to record the **start** and **end** time to retrieve the elapsed time by subtracting the end value with the start value. In addition to the elapsed time of each Fetch() method invocation, we also calculate the elapsed time of the entire code. The implementation of the not_optimize_code.cpp code is as follows:

```cpp
/* not_optimize_code.cpp */
#include <iostream>
#include <functional>
#include <chrono>

using namespace std;

template<class T> class Delay
{
  private:
    function<T()> m_func;
```

```
    public:
      Delay(function<T()> func): m_func(func)
      {
      }

      T Fetch()
      {
        return m_func();
      }
};

// Function for calculating Fibonacci sequence
int fibonacci(int n)
{
  if(n <= 1)
      return n;
  return fibonacci(n-1) + fibonacci(n-2);
}

auto main() -> int
{
  cout << "[not_optimize_code.cpp]" << endl;
  // Recording start time for the program
  auto start = chrono::high_resolution_clock::now();
  // Initializing int variable to store the result
  // from Fibonacci calculation
  int fib40Result = 0;

  // Constructing Delay<> named fib40
  Delay<int> fib40([]()
  {
    return fibonacci(40);
  });

  for (int i = 1; i <= 5; ++i)
  {
    cout << "Invocation " << i << ". ";

    // Recording start time
    auto start = chrono::high_resolution_clock::now();

    // Invoking the Fetch() method
    // in fib40 instance
    fib40Result = fib40.Fetch();

    // Recording end time
    auto finish = chrono::high_resolution_clock::now();
```

```
        // Calculating the elapsed time
        chrono::duration<double, milli> elapsed = finish - start;

        // Displaying the result
        cout << "Result = " << fib40Result << ". ";

        // Displaying elapsed time
        // for each fib40.Fetch() invocation
        cout << "Consuming time = " << elapsed.count();
        cout << " milliseconds" << endl;
    }

    // Recording end time for the program
    auto finish = chrono::high_resolution_clock::now();

    // Calculating the elapsed time for the program
    chrono::duration<double, milli> elapsed = finish - start;

    // Displaying elapsed time for the program
    cout << "Total consuming time = ";
    cout << elapsed.count() << " milliseconds" << endl;

    return 0;
}
```

Now, let's run the code to obtain the elapsed time of the preceding code process. The following screenshot is what we will see on the screen:

```
[not_optimize_code.cpp]
Invocation 1. Result = 102334155. Consuming time = 468.333 microseconds
Invocation 2. Result = 102334155. Consuming time = 471.845 microseconds
Invocation 3. Result = 102334155. Consuming time = 470.331 microseconds
Invocation 4. Result = 102334155. Consuming time = 470.331 microseconds
Invocation 5. Result = 102334155. Consuming time = 472.336 microseconds
Total consuming time = 2357.79 microseconds
```

From the preceding screenshot, we can see that we need about 2357.79 milliseconds to process the code. And each time it invokes the fib40.Fetch() method, it needs an average of about 470 milliseconds, although we pass the exact same argument to the fibonacci() function, which is 40. Now, let's see what will happen if we use the memoization technique on the preceding code. We won't modify the code much, just refactor the instantiation of fib40. Instead of instancing from the Delay class, now it instances from the Memoization class. The code should be as follows:

```
/* optimizing_memoization.cpp */
#include <iostream>
#include <functional>
#include <chrono>

using namespace std;

template<class T> class Memoization
{
  private:
    T const & (*m_subRoutine)(Memoization *);
    mutable T m_recordedFunc;
    function<T()> m_func;

    static T const & ForceSubroutine(Memoization * d)
    {
      return d->DoRecording();
    }

    static T const & FetchSubroutine(Memoization * d)
    {
      return d->FetchRecording();
    }

    T const & FetchRecording()
    {
      return m_recordedFunc;
    }

    T const & DoRecording()
    {
      m_recordedFunc = m_func();
      m_subRoutine = &FetchSubroutine;
      return FetchRecording();
    }

  public:
    Memoization(function<T()> func): m_func(func),
      m_subRoutine(&ForceSubroutine),
```

```
        m_recordedFunc(T())
        {
        }

    T Fetch()
    {
        return m_subRoutine(this);
    }
};

    // Function for calculating Fibonacci sequence
    int fibonacci(int n)
    {
      if(n <= 1)
        return n;
        return fibonacci(n-1) + fibonacci(n-2);
    }

    auto main() -> int
    {
      cout << "[optimizing_memoization.cpp]" << endl;

      // Recording start time for the program
      auto start = chrono::high_resolution_clock::now();

      // Initializing int variable to store the result
      // from Fibonacci calculation
      int fib40Result = 0;

      // Constructing Memoization<> named fib40
      Memoization<int> fib40([]()
      {
        return fibonacci(40);
      });

      for (int i = 1; i <= 5; ++i)
      {
        cout << "Invocation " << i << ". ";

        // Recording start time
        auto start = chrono::high_resolution_clock::now();

        // Invoking the Fetch() method
        // in fib40 instance
        fib40Result = fib40.Fetch();

        // Recording end time
        auto finish = chrono::high_resolution_clock::now();
```

```
        // Calculating the elapsed time
        chrono::duration<double, milli> elapsed = finish - start;

        // Displaying the result
        cout << "Result = " << fib40Result << ". ";

        // Displaying elapsed time
        // for each fib40.Fetch() invocation
        cout << "Consuming time = " << elapsed.count();
        cout << " milliseconds" << endl;
    }

    // Recording end time for the program
    auto finish = chrono::high_resolution_clock::now();

    // Calculating the elapsed time for the program
    chrono::duration<double, milli> elapsed = finish - start;

    // Displaying elapsed time for the program
    cout << "Total consuming time = ";
    cout << elapsed.count() << " milliseconds" << endl;

    return 0;
}
```

Here is what we'll get on the console screen when we run the
`optimizing_memoization.cpp` code:

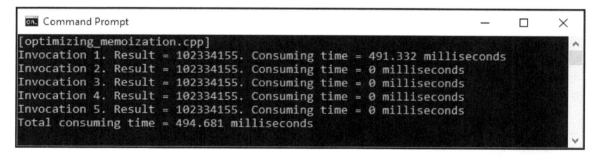

Surprisingly, we just need `494.681` milliseconds to execute the
`optimizing_memoization.cpp` code. Compared to the `not_optimize_code.cpp` code,
the speed of the code is about `4.7` times faster. This happens because the code successfully
cached the result of the `fibonacci()` function when it passed the `40` to its parameter. Each
time we call the `fib40.Fetch()` method again, it will invoke the `fibonacci()` function
again, with the exact same input. The code will just return the cached result so it can avoid
running the expensive function calls that are unnecessary to run.

Lazy evaluation in action

Having discussed the basic concept of lazy evaluation, let's dig into lazy evaluation by designing the code in the lazy approach. In this section, we will develop an eager evaluation code first, then refactor that code into the lazy evaluation one. The code we develop will generate a sequence of prime numbers. First, we will use the `for` loop to iterate the integer number to obtain the prime number in the eager evaluation. The following `prime.cpp` code is what we are talking about:

```cpp
/* prime.cpp */
#include <iostream>
#include <cmath>

using namespace std;

bool PrimeCheck(int i)
{
  // All even numbers are not prime number
  // except 2
  if ((i % 2) == 0)
  {
    return i == 2;
  }

  // Calculating the square root of i
  // and store in int data type variable
  // if the argument i is not even number,
  int sqr = sqrt(i);

  // For numbers 9 and below,
  // the prime numbers is simply the odd numbers
  // For number above 9
  // the prime numbers is all of odd numbers
  // except the square number
  for (int t = 3; t <= sqr; t += 2)
  {
    if (i % t == 0)
    {
        return false;
    }
  }

  // The number 1 is not prime number
  // but still passing the preceding test
  return i != 1;
}
```

```
auto main() -> int
{
  cout << "[delaying.cpp]" << endl;

  // Initializing a counting variable
  int n = 0;

  // Displaying the first 100 prime numbers
  cout << "List of the first 100 prime numbers:" << endl;
  for (int i = 0; ; ++i)
  {
    if (PrimeCheck(i))
    {
        cout << i << "\t";

        if (++n == 100)
            return 0;
    }
  }

  return 0;
}
```

As we can see in the preceding code, we have a simple `PrimeCheck()` function to analyze whether the integer number is a prime number or not. Afterward, the code iterates the infinity integer numbers using the `for` loop, then checks whether it's a prime number. The loop will be ended if we've got one hundred prime numbers. The following screenshot is the output on the console we should see:

We now have a code generating prime numbers using eager evaluation. As we can see in the preceding screenshot, we have a hundred prime numbers that we generated using the `for` loop. Next, we will refactor it into the lazy code.

Designing Chunk and Row classes

In the `prime.cpp` code, we generate a row of integer numbers using the `for` loop. In this row, there are several numbers that are called **Chunk**. Now, before we refactor the code, we will prepare a class named `Row` and `Chunk` for our further discussion. From our preceding analogy, the `Row` class will hold the sequence of integer number and the `Chunk` class will hold a single number. We will start with the smallest part in the data, which is the chunk. And here is the implementation of the `Chunk` class:

```cpp
template<class T> class Chunk
{
  private:
    T m_value;
    Row<T> m_lastRow;

  public:
    Chunk()
    {
    }

    Chunk(T value, Row<T> lastRow): m_value(value),
     m_lastRow(std::move(lastRow))
    {
    }

    explicit Chunk(T value) : m_value(value)
    {
    }

    T Value() const
    {
      return m_value;
    }

    Row<T> ShiftLastToFirst() const
    {
      return m_lastRow;
    }
};
```

Since the `Row` class is constructed from several `Chunk` classes, besides the value of `Chunk` itself, the `Chunk` class also has the next value of `Chunk` in the current `Row` notated by the `m_lastRow` member variable. We also can get the `m_lastRow` value by invoking the `ShiftLastToFirst()` method. Now, let's move to the `Row` class. The implementation of the class is as follows:

```cpp
template<class T> class Row
{
  private:
    std::shared_ptr <Memoization<Chunk<T>>>
    m_lazyChunk;

  public:
    Row()
    {
    }

    explicit Row(T value)
    {
      auto chunk = ChunkPreparation<T>(value);
      m_lazyChunk = std::make_shared<Memoization<Chunk<T>>>
      (chunk);
    }

    Row(T value, Row row)
    {
      auto chunk = ChunkPreparation<T>( value, std::move(row));

      m_lazyChunk = std::make_shared<Memoization<Chunk<T>>>(
      chunk);
    }
    Row(std::function<Chunk<T>()> func): m_lazyChunk(
    std::make_shared<Memoization<Chunk<T>>>(func))
    {
    }

    bool IsEmpty() const
    {
      return !m_lazyChunk;
    }
    T Fetch() const
    {
      return m_lazyChunk->Fetch().Value();
    }

    Row<T> ShiftLastToFirst() const
    {
```

```
      return m_lazyChunk->Fetch().ShiftLastToFirst();
    }

    Row Pick(int n) const
    {
      if (n == 0 || IsEmpty())
        return Row();

    auto chunk = m_lazyChunk;
    return Row([chunk, n]()
    {
      auto val = chunk->Fetch().Value();
      auto row = chunk->Fetch().ShiftLastToFirst();
      return Chunk<T>(val, row.Pick(n - 1));
    });
    }
};
```

As we can see in the preceding code snippet, the Row class has only one private member to store a memoization of the Chunk data. There are four constructors the Row class has, and we will use them all in our next code. It also has the Fetch() method, which we got when we designed the Memoization class in the previous section, to get the m_lazyChunk value. The other methods are also useful to our next lazy code. The IsEmpty() method will check if the m_lazyChunk value is empty, the ShiftLastToFirst() method will take the last row of m_lazyChunk, and the Pick(int n) method will take out the first n row's elements that we will use if we need to take out a hundred of the integer prime numbers later.

We can also see that one of the Row constructors is invoking the ChunkPreparation class constructor. The ChunkPreparation class will initialize a new Chunk class constructor using the given value and the last row value. The implementation of the class is as follows:

```
template<class T> class ChunkPreparation
{
  public:
    T m_value;
    Row<T> m_row;

    ChunkPreparation(T value, Row<T> row) :
      m_value(value),
      m_row(std::move(row))
      {
      }

    explicit ChunkPreparation(T value) :
      m_value(value)
      {
```

```
        }

        Chunk<T> operator()()
        {
          return Chunk<T>(
            m_value,
            m_row);
        }
    };
```

As we can see, by invoking `operator ()`, the new `Chunk` will be generated with the given `m_value` and `m_row` value.

Concatenating several rows

When we plan to generate a row of prime numbers, we have to be able to concatenate the current with the new row generated by code. To address this need, the following is the implementation of the `ConcatenateRows()` function that will concatenate the two rows:

```
template<class T> Row<T> ConcatenateRows(
  Row<T> leftRow,
  Row<T> rightRow)
{
  if (leftRow.IsEmpty())
    return rightRow;

  return Row<T>([=]()
  {
    return Chunk<T>(
      leftRow.Fetch(),
      ConcatenateRows<T>(
       leftRow.ShiftLastToFirst(),
       rightRow));
  });
}
```

It's quite clear what the `ConcatenateRows()` function does when we take a look at the preceding code snippet. If `leftRow` is still empty, just return the second row, which is `rightRow`. If `leftRow` and `rightRow` is available, we can return the chunks of the given rows that have been formed as a row.

Iterating each Row class' element

After we construct the row of prime numbers, we need to iterate each row's element to manipulate it, for instance, to print the value to the console. For this purpose, we have to develop the following `ForEach()` method:

```
template<class T, class U> void ForEach( Row<T> row, U func)
  {
    while (!row.IsEmpty())
    {
      func(row.Fetch());
      row = row.ShiftLastToFirst();
    }
  }
```

We will pass the row itself and a function into the `ForEach()` method. The function we passed to it will be run to each element of the row.

 For our convenience in developing the lazy code in this chapter, I will bundle our previous discussion `template` class into a single header file named `lazyevaluation.h`; we can also reuse it for other projects. The header will contain the `Memoization`, `Row`, `Chunk`, `ChunkPreparation`, `ConcatenateRows`, and `ForEach` template class. You can create the header file yourself or download it from the code repository on the Packt website (`https://github.com/PacktPublishing/LearningCPPFunction alProgramming`).

Generating the infinite integer row

Now it's time to generating the infinite integer row as we did using the `for` loop in our previous `prime.cpp` code. However, we will now create a new function named `GenerateInfiniteIntRow()` to generate an integer row from several integer chunks. The following code snippet is an implementation of the function:

```
Row<int> GenerateInfiniteIntRow( int initialNumber)
  {
    return Row<int>([initialNumber]()
    {
      return Chunk<int>(
          initialNumber,
          GenerateInfinityIntRow(
            initialNumber + 1));
    });
```

```
      }
```

As we can see, first, we create `Chunk` from `initialNumber` until infinity. The chunks will be transformed to the `Row` data type at the end. To stop this recursive function, we can call the `Pick()` method inside the `Row` class.

Generating an infinite prime numbers row

After successfully generated infinite numbers, we now have to limit the row to only generate the prime number. We will modify the `CheckPrime()` function from the `prime.cpp` code. We will change the return value of the function, `Row<void*>(nullptr)` if it's not a prime number or `Row<void*>()` if the opposite. The implementation of the function should be as follows:

```
Row<void*> PrimeCheck(int i)
{
  if ((i % 2) == 0)
  {
    if (i == 2)
        return Row<void*>(nullptr);
    else
        return Row<void*>();
  }

  int sqr = sqrt(i);

  for (int t = 3; t <= sqr; t = t + 2)
  {
    if (i % t == 0)
    {
        return Row<void*>();
    }
  }

  if (i == 1)
    return Row<void*>();
  else
    return Row<void*>(nullptr);
}
```

Why do we need to change the return value of the function? Because we want to pass the return value to the `JoiningPrimeNumber()` function, which will join the generated Chunk with the following implementation:

```
template<class T, class U>
auto JoiningPrimeNumber(
  Row<T> row, U func) -> decltype(func())
  {
      return JoiningAllRows(
        MappingRowByValue(row, func));
  }
```

Moreover, the `MappingRowByValue()` function will map the given row to the given function. The implementation of the function is as follows:

```
template<class T, class U>
auto MappingRowByValue(
  Row<T> row, U func) -> Row<decltype(func())>
{
  using V = decltype(func());

  if (row.IsEmpty())
    return Row<V>();

  return Row<V>([row, func]()
  {
    return Chunk<V>(
      func(),
      MappingRowByValue(
        row.ShiftLastToFirst(),
        func));
  });
}
```

After we have successfully joined all prime numbers using the `JoiningPrimeNumber()` function, we have to bind it to the existing row using the `Binding()` function with the following implementation:

```
template<class T, class U> Row<T>
Binding( Row<T> row, U func)
{
    return JoiningAllRows( MappingRow( row, func));
}
```

From the preceding code snippet, the `MappingRow()` function will map the given row to the given function, then `JoiningAllRows()` will join all rows from the `MappingRow()` return value. The implementation of the `MappingRow()` and `JoiningAllRows()` functions are as follows:

```
template<class T, class U>
auto MappingRow(
  Row<T> row, U func) -> Row<decltype(
    func(row.Fetch()))>
  {
    using V = decltype(func(row.Fetch()));

    if (row.IsEmpty())
      return Row<V>();

    return Row<V>([row, func]()
    {
      return Chunk<V>(func(
        row.Fetch()),
        MappingRow(
          row.ShiftLastToFirst(),
          func));
    });
  }

template<class T> Row<T>
JoiningAllRows(
  Row<Row<T>> rowOfRows)
{
  while (!rowOfRows.IsEmpty() &&
    rowOfRows.Fetch().IsEmpty())
  {
    rowOfRows = rowOfRows.ShiftLastToFirst();
  }

  if (rowOfRows.IsEmpty())
    return Row<T>();

  return Row<T>([rowOfRows]()
  {
    Row<T> row = rowOfRows.Fetch();

    return Chunk<T>(
      row.Fetch(),
      ConcatenateRows(
        row.ShiftLastToFirst(),
        JoiningAllRows(
```

```
                rowOfRows.ShiftLastToFirst())));
    });
}
```

Now we can create a function to limit the infinite integer number rows with the following implementation:

```
Row<int> GenerateInfinitePrimeRow()
{
  return Binding(
    GenerateInfiniteIntRow(1),
    [](int i)
    {
      return JoiningPrimeNumber(
        PrimeCheck(i),
        [i]()
        {
          return ConvertChunkToRow(i);
        });
    });
}
```

Since the second argument of the `JoiningPrimeNumber()` function needs a row as a data type, we need to convert the `Chunk` to `Row` using the `ConvertChunkToRow()` function with the following implementations:

```
template<class T> Row<T>
ConvertChunkToRow(
  T value)
  {
    return Row<T>([value]()
    {
      return Chunk<T>(value);
    });
  }
```

Now we can consume all preceding classes and functions to refactor our `prime.cpp` code.

Refactoring eager evaluation to lazy evaluation

We have all the functions we need to refactor the `prime.cpp` code into a lazy code. We will create a `prime_lazy.cpp` code that will generate infinite integer numbers first and pick the first one hundred of its elements. After that, we iterate a hundred elements and give them to the function that will print the value on the console. The code should look like this:

```cpp
/* prime_lazy.cpp */
#include <iostream>
#include <cmath>
#include "../lazyevaluation/lazyevaluation.h"

using namespace std;

Row<void*> PrimeCheck(int i)
{
  // Use preceding implementation
}

Row<int> GenerateInfiniteIntRow(
  int initialNumber)
{
  // Use preceding implementation
}

template<class T, class U>
auto MappingRow(
  Row<T> row, U func) -> Row<decltype(
    func(row.Fetch()))>
  {
    // Use preceding implementation
  }

template<class T, class U>
auto MappingRowByValue(
  Row<T> row, U func) -> Row<decltype(func())>
  {
    // Use preceding implementation
  }

template<class T> Row<T>
ConvertChunkToRow(
  T value)
{
  // Use preceding implementation
}
```

```
template<class T> Row<T>
JoiningAllRows(
  Row<Row<T>> rowOfRows)
{
  // Use preceding implementation
}

template<class T, class U> Row<T>
Binding(
  Row<T> row, U func)
  {
    // Use preceding implementation
  }

template<class T, class U>
auto JoiningPrimeNumber(
  Row<T> row, U func) -> decltype(func())
  {
    // Use preceding implementation
  }

Row<int> GenerateInfinitePrimeRow()
{
  // Use preceding implementation
}

auto main() -> int
{
  cout << "[prime_lazy.cpp]" << endl;

  // Generating infinite prime numbers list
  Row<int> r = GenerateInfinitePrimeRow();

  // Picking the first 100 elements from preceding list
  Row<int> firstAHundredPrimeNumbers = r.Pick(100);

  // Displaying the first 100 prime numbers
  cout << "List of the first 100 prime numbers:" << endl;
  ForEach(
    move(firstAHundredPrimeNumbers),
    [](int const & i)
    {
        cout << i << "\t";
    });

  return 0;
}
```

As we can see from the preceding code, we have `r` that holds the infinite numbers, then we pick the first one hundred prime numbers and store them to `firstAHundredPrimeNumbers`. To print the value of the element to the console, we use the `ForEach()` function and pass the Lambda expression to it. If we run the code, the result is exactly the same as the `prime.cpp` code, except the title that is used is a differentiator. The following output is what we should see on the console if we run the `prime_lazy.cpp` code:

```
Command Prompt                                           —   □   ×
[prime_lazy.cpp]
List of the first 100 prime numbers:
2      3      5      7      11     13     17     19     23     29
31     37     41     43     47     53     59     61     67     71
73     79     83     89     97     101    103    107    109    113
127    131    137    139    149    151    157    163    167    173
179    181    191    193    197    199    211    223    227    229
233    239    241    251    257    263    269    271    277    281
283    293    307    311    313    317    331    337    347    349
353    359    367    373    379    383    389    397    401    409
419    421    431    433    439    443    449    457    461    463
467    479    487    491    499    503    509    521    523    541
```

By using the `template` class, we have revealed in this chapter that we can develop other lazy code to gain the benefit of being lazy.

> In the preceding `prime_lazy.cpp` code, I omitted several lines of code that were written in the previous section to avoid the code redundancy. If you find any difficulty following the code because it's not complete, go to https://github.com/PacktPublishing/LearningCPPFunctionalProgramming.

Summary

Lazy evaluation is not only useful for functional programming, but it actually also has benefits for imperative programming. Using the lazy evaluation, we can have an efficient and faster code by implementing caching and optimizing techniques.

In the next chapter, we will talk about metaprogramming that we can use in the functional approach. We will discuss how to use metaprogramming to gain all its benefits, including code optimization.

6
Optimizing Code with Metaprogramming

We discussed the optimizing techniques using lazy evaluation in the previous chapter, and used the delaying process, caching technique, and memoization to make our code run fast. In this chapter, we will optimize the code using **metaprogramming**, where we will create a code that will create more code. The topics we will discuss in this chapter are as follows:

- Introduction to metaprogramming
- The part that builds the template metaprogramming
- Refactoring flow control into template metaprogramming
- Running the code in the compile-time execution
- The advantages and disadvantages of template metaprogramming

Introduction to metaprogramming

The simplest way to say this is that metaprogramming is a technique that creates a code by using a code. Implementing metaprogramming, we write a computer program that manipulates the other programs and treats them as its data. In addition, templates are a compile-time mechanism in C++ that is **Turing-complete**, which means any computation expressible by a computer program can be computed, in some form, by a template metaprogram before runtime. It also uses recursion a lot and has immutable variables. So, in metaprogramming, we create code that will run when the code is compiled.

Preprocessing the code using a macro

To start our discussion on metaprogramming, let's go back to the era when the ANSI C programming language was a popular language. For simplicity, we used the C preprocessor by creating a macro. The C parameterized macro is also known as **metafunctions**, and is one of the examples of metaprogramming. Consider the following parameterized macro:

```
#define MAX(a,b) (((a) > (b)) ? (a) : (b))
```

Since the C++ programming language has a drawback compatibility to the C language, we can compile the preceding macro using our C++ compiler. Let's create the code to consume the preceding macro, which will be as follows:

```cpp
/* macro.cpp */
#include <iostream>

using namespace std;

// Defining macro
#define MAX(a,b) (((a) > (b)) ? (a) : (b))

auto main() -> int
{
  cout << "[macro.cpp]" << endl;

  // Initializing two int variables
  int x = 10;
  int y = 20;

  // Consuming the MAX macro
  // and assign the result to z variable
  int z = MAX(x,y);

  // Displaying the result
  cout << "Max number of " << x << " and " << y;
  cout << " is " << z << endl;

  return 0;
}
```

As we can see in the preceding `macro.cpp` code, we pass two arguments to the `MAX` macro since it is a parameterized macro, which means the parameter can be obtained from the users. If we run the preceding code, we should see the following output on the console:

As we discussed at the beginning of this chapter, metaprogramming is a code that will run in compile time. By using a macro in the preceding code, we can demonstrate there's a new code generated from the `MAX` macro. The preprocessor will parse the macro in compile time and bring the new code. In compile time, the compiler modifies the code as follows:

```
auto main() -> int
{
    // same code
    // ...
    int z = (((a) > (b)) ? (a) : (b)); // <-- Notice this section

    // same code
    // ...

    return 0;
}
```

Besides a one line macro preprocessor, we can also generate a multiline macro metafunction. To achieve this, we can use the backslash character at the end of the line. Let's suppose we need to swap the two values. We can create a parameterized macro named `SWAP` and consume it like the following code:

```
/* macroswap.cpp */
#include <iostream>

using namespace std;

// Defining multi line macro
#define SWAP(a,b) { \
    (a) ^= (b); \
    (b) ^= (a); \
    (a) ^= (b); \
}

auto main() -> int
{
```

```
    cout << "[macroswap.cpp]" << endl;

    // Initializing two int variables
    int x = 10;
    int y = 20;

    // Displaying original variable value
    cout << "before swapping" << endl;
    cout << "x = " << x << ", y = " << y ;
    cout << endl << endl;

    // Consuming the SWAP macro
    SWAP(x,y);

    // Displaying swapped variable value
    cout << "after swapping" << endl;
    cout << "x = " << x << ", y = " << y;
    cout << endl;

    return 0;
}
```

As we can see in the preceding code, we will create a multiline preprocessor macro and use backslash characters at the end of each line. Each time we invoke the SWAP parameterized macro, it will then be replaced with the implementation of the macro. We will see the following output on the console if we run the preceding code:

Now we have a basic understanding of the metaprogramming, especially in metafunction, we can move further in the next topics.

We use parenthesis for each variable in every implementation of the macro preprocessor because the preprocessor is simply replacing our code with the implementation of the macro. Let's suppose we have the following macro:

```
MULTIPLY(a,b) (a * b)
```

It won't be a problem if we pass the number as the parameters. However, if we pass an operation as the argument, a problem will occur. For instance, if we use the MULTIPLY macro as follows:

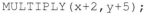

```
MULTIPLY(x+2,y+5);
```

Then the compiler will replace it as (x+2*y+5). This happens because the macro just replaces the a variable with the x + 2 expression and the b variable with the y + 5 expression, with any additional parentheses. And because the order of multiplication is higher than addition, we will have got the result as follows:

```
(x+2y+5)
```

And that is not what we expect. As a result, the best approach is to use parenthesis in each variable of the parameter.

Dissecting template metaprogramming in the Standard Library

We discussed the Standard Library in Chapter 1, *Diving into Modern C++*, and dealt with it in the previous chapter too. The Standard Library provided in the C++ language is mostly a template that contains an incomplete function. However, it will be used to generate complete functions. The template metaprogramming is the C++ template to generate C++ types and code in compile time.

Let's pick up one of the classes in the Standard Library--the `Array` class. In the `Array` class, we can define a data type for it. When we instance the array, the compiler actually generates the code for an array of the data type we define. Now, let's try to build a simple `Array` template implementation as follows:

```
template<typename T>
class Array
{
  T element;
};
```

Then, we instance the `char` and `int` arrays as follows:

```
Array<char> arrChar;
Array<int> arrInt;
```

What the compiler does is it creates these two implementations of the template based on the data type we define. Although we won't see this in the code, the compiler actually creates the following code:

```
class ArrayChar
{
  char element;
};

class ArrayInt
{
  int element;
};

ArrayChar arrChar;
ArrayInt arrInt;
```

As we can see in the preceding code snippet, the template metaprogramming is a code that creates another code in compile time.

Building the template metaprogramming

Before we go further in the template metaprogramming discussion, it's better if we discuss the skeleton that builds the template metaprogramming. There are four factors that form the template metaprogramming--**type**, **value**, **branch**, and **recursion**. In this topic, we will dig into the factors that form the template.

Adding a value to the variable in the template

At the beginning of this chapter, we discussed the concept of metafunction when we talked about the macro preprocessor. In the macro preprocessor, we explicitly manipulate the source code; in this case, the macro (metafunction) manipulates the source code. In contrast, we work with types in C++ template metaprogramming. This means the metafunction is a function that works with types. So, the better approach to use template metaprogramming is working with type parameters only when possible. When we are talking about the variables in template metaprogramming, it's actually not a variable since the value on it cannot be modified. What we need from the variable is its name so we can access it. Because we will code with types, the named values are `typedef`, as we can see in the following code snippet:

```
struct ValueDataType
{
  typedef int valueDataType;
};
```

By using the preceding code, we store the `int` type to the `valueDataType` alias name so we can access the data type using the `valueDataType` variable. If we need to store a value instead of the data type to the variable, we can use `enum` so it will be the data member of the `enum` itself. Let's take a look at the following code snippet if we want to store the value:

```
struct ValuePlaceHolder
{
  enum
    {
     value = 1
    };
};
```

Based on the preceding code snippet, we can now access the `value` variable to fetch its value.

Mapping a function to the input parameters

We can add the variable to the template metaprogramming. Now, what we have to do next is retrieve the user parameters and map them to a function. Let's suppose we want to develop a `Multiplexer` function that will multiply two values and we have to use the template metaprogramming. The following code snippet can be used to solve this problem:

```
template<int A, int B>
struct Multiplexer
```

```
  {
    enum
    {
      result = A * B
    };
  };
```

As we can see in the preceding code snippet, the template requires two arguments, A and B, from the user, and it will use them to get the value of `result` variable by multiplying these two parameters. We can access the result variable using the following code:

```
int i = Multiplexer<2, 3>::result;
```

If we run the preceding code snippet, the i variable will store 6 since it will calculate 2 times 3.

Choosing the correct process based on the condition

When we have more than one function, we have to choose one over the others based on certain conditions. We can construct the conditional branch by providing two alternative specializations of the `template` class, as shown here:

```
template<typename A, typename B>
struct CheckingType
{
  enum
  {
    result = 0
  };
};

template<typename X>
struct CheckingType<X, X>
{
  enum
  {
    result = 1
  };
};
```

As we can see in the preceding `template` code, we have two templates that have X and A/B as their type. When the template has only a single type, that is, `typename X`, it means that the two types (`CheckingType <X, X>`) we compare are exactly the same. Otherwise, these two data types are different. The following code snippet can be used to consume the two preceding templates:

```
if (CheckingType<UnknownType, int>::result)
{
  // run the function if the UnknownType is int
}
else
{
  // otherwise run any function
}
```

As we can see in the preceding code snippet, we try to compare the `UnknownType` data type with the `int` type. The `UnknownType` data type might be coming from the other process. Then, we can decide the next process we want to run by comparing these two types using templates.

 Up to here, you might wonder how template multiprogramming will help us make code optimization. Soon we will use the template metaprogramming to optimize code. However, we need to discuss other things that will solidify our knowledge in template multiprogramming. For now, please be patient and keep reading.

Repeating the process recursively

We have successfully added value and data type to the template, then created a branch to decide the next process based on the current condition. Another thing we have to consider in the basic template is repeating the process. However, since the variable in the template is immutable, we cannot iterate the sequence. Instead, we have to recur the process as we discussed in `Chapter 4`, *Repeating Method Invocation Using Recursive Algorithm*.

Let's suppose we are developing a template to calculate the factorial value. The first thing we have to do is develop a general template that passes the I value to the function as follows:

```
template <int I>
struct Factorial
{
  enum
  {
    value = I * Factorial<I-1>::value
```

```
    };
};
```

As we can see in the preceding code, we can obtain the value of the factorial by running the following code:

```
Factorial<I>::value;
```

In the preceding code, I is an integer number.

Next, we have to develop a template to ensure that it doesn't end up with an infinite loop. We can create the following template that passes zero (0) as a parameter to it:

```
template <>
struct Factorial<0>
{
  enum
  {
    value = 1
  };
};
```

Now we have a pair of templates that will generate the value of the factorial in compile time. The following is a sample code to get the value of Factorial(10) in compile time:

```
int main()
{
  int fact10 = Factorial<10>::value;
}
```

If we run the preceding code, we will get 3628800 as a result of the factorial of 10.

Selecting a type in compile-time

As we discussed in the preceding topic, type is a basic part of a template. However, we can select a certain type based on the input from the user. Let's create a template that can decide what type should be used in the variable. The following types.cpp code will show the implementation of the template:

```
/* types.cpp */
#include <iostream>

using namespace std;

// Defining a data type
// in template
```

```
template<typename T>
struct datatype
{
  using type = T;
};

auto main() -> int
{
  cout << "[types.cpp]" << endl;

  // Selecting a data type in compile time
  using t = typename datatype<int>::type;

  // Using the selected data type
  t myVar = 123;

  // Displaying the selected data type
  cout << "myVar = " << myVar;

  return 0;
}
```

As we can see in the preceding code, we have a template named datatype. This template can be used to select the type we pass to it. We can use the using keyword to assign a variable to a type. From the preceding types.cpp code, we will assign a t variable to type from the datatype template. The t variable now will be int since we passed the int data type to the template.

We can also create a code to select the correct data type based on the current condition. We will have an IfElseDataType template that takes three arguments which are predicate, the data type when the predicate parameter is true, and the data type when the predicate parameter is false. The code will look as follows:

```
/* selectingtype.cpp */
#include <iostream>

using namespace std;

// Defining IfElseDataType template
template<
  bool predicate,
  typename TrueType,
  typename FalseType>
  struct IfElseDataType
  {
  };
```

```cpp
// Defining template for TRUE condition
// passed to 'predicate' parameter
template<
  typename TrueType,
  typename FalseType>
  struct IfElseDataType<
   true,
   TrueType,
   FalseType>
   {
     typedef TrueType type;
   };

// Defining template for FALSE condition
// passed to 'predicate' parameter
template<
  typename TrueType,
  typename FalseType>
  struct IfElseDataType<
  false,
  TrueType,
  FalseType>
  {
     typedef FalseType type;
  };

auto main() -> int
{
  cout << "[types.cpp]" << endl;

  // Consuming template and passing
  // 'SHRT_MAX == 2147483647'
  // It will be FALSE
  // since the maximum value of short
  // is 32767
  // so the data type for myVar
  // will be 'int'
  IfElseDataType<
    SHRT_MAX == 2147483647,
    short,
    int>::type myVar;

  // Assigning myVar to maximum value
  // of 'short' type
  myVar = 2147483647;

  // Displaying the data type of myVar
  cout << "myVar has type ";
```

```
    cout << typeid(myVar).name() << endl;

    return 0;
}
```

Now, by having the `IfElseDataType` template, we can select the correct type to the variable based on the condition we have. Let's suppose we want to assign `2147483647` to a variable so we can check if it's a short number. If so, `myVar` will be of type `short`, otherwise, it will be `int`. Moreover, since the maximum value of `short` type is `32767`, by giving the predicate as `SHRT_MAX == 2147483647` will be resulting `FALSE`. Therefore, the type of `myVar` will be an `int` type, as we can see in the following output that will appear on the console:

Flow control with template metaprogramming

Code flow is an important aspect in coding a program. In many programming languages, they have an `if-else`, `switch`, and `do-while` statement to arrange the flow of the code. Now, let's refactor the usual flow of code to become a template-based flow. We will start by using the `if-else` statement, followed by the `switch` statement, and finally ending with the `do-while` statement, all in templates.

Deciding the next process by the current condition

Now it's time to use the template as we discussed previously. Let's suppose we have two functions that we have to choose by a certain condition. What we usually do is use the `if-else` statement as follows:

```
/* condition.cpp */
#include <iostream>

using namespace std;
```

```
// Function that will run
// if the condition is TRUE
void TrueStatement()
{
  cout << "True Statement is run." << endl;
}

// Function that will run
// if the condition is FALSE
void FalseStatement()
{
  cout << "False Statement is run." << endl;
}

auto main() -> int
{
  cout << "[condition.cpp]" << endl;

  // Choosing the function
  // based on the condition
  if (2 + 3 == 5)
    TrueStatement();
  else
    FalseStatement();

  return 0;
}
```

As we can see in the preceding code, we have two functions--TrueStatement() and FalseStatement(). We also have a condition in the code--2 + 3 == 5. And since the condition is TRUE, then the TrueStatement() function will be run as we can see in the following screenshot:

Now, let's refactor the preceding condition.cpp code. We will create three templates here. First, the template initialization that inputs the condition as follows:

```
template<bool predicate> class IfElse
```

Then, we create two templates for each condition--TRUE or FALSE. The name will be as follows:

```
template<> class IfElse<true>
template<> class IfElse<false>
```

Each template in the preceding code snippet will run the functions we have created before--the TrueStatement() and FalseStatement() functions. And we will get the complete code as the following conditionmeta.cpp code:

```
/* conditionmeta.cpp */
#include <iostream>

using namespace std;

// Function that will run
// if the condition is TRUE
void TrueStatement()
{
  cout << "True Statement is run." << endl;
}

// Function that will run
// if the condition is FALSE
void FalseStatement()
{
  cout << "False Statement is run." << endl;
}

// Defining IfElse template
template<bool predicate>
class IfElse
{
};

// Defining template for TRUE condition
// passed to 'predicate' parameter
template<>
class IfElse<true>
{
  public:
    static inline void func()
    {
      TrueStatement();
    }
};

// Defining template for FALSE condition
```

```
      // passed to 'predicate' parameter
      template<>
      class IfElse<false>
      {
        public:
          static inline void func()
          {
            FalseStatement();
          }
      };

      auto main() -> int
      {
        cout << "[conditionmeta.cpp]" << endl;

        // Consuming IfElse template
        IfElse<(2 + 3 == 5)>::func();

        return 0;
      }
```

As we can see, we put the condition on the bracket of the IfElse template, then call the func() method inside the template. If we run the conditionmeta.cpp code, we will get the exact same output such as the condition.cpp code, as shown here:

We now have the if-else statement to flow our code in the template metaprogramming.

Selecting the correct statement

In C++ programming, and other programming languages as well, we use the switch statement to select a certain process based on the value we give to the switch statement. If the value matches with the one of the switch case, it will run the process under that case. Let's take a look at the following switch.cpp code that implements the switch statement:

```
      /* switch.cpp */
      #include <iostream>

      using namespace std;
```

```cpp
// Function to find out
// the square of an int
int Square(int a)
{
  return a * a;
}

auto main() -> int
{
  cout << "[switch.cpp]" << endl;

  // Initializing two int variables
  int input = 2;
  int output = 0;

  // Passing the correct argument
  // to the function
  switch (input)
  {
    case 1:
        output = Square(1);
        break;
    case 2:
        output = Square(2);
        break;
    default:
        output = Square(0);
        break;
  }

  // Displaying the result
  cout << "The result is " << output << endl;

  return 0;
}
```

As we can see in the preceding code, we have a function named Square() that takes an argument. The argument we pass to it is based on the value that we give to the switch statement. Since the value we pass to switch is 2, the Square(2) method will be run. The following screenshot is what we will see on the console screen:

To refactor the `switch.cpp` code to template metaprogramming, we have to create three templates that consist of the function we plan to run. First, we will create the initialization template to retrieve the value from the user, as follows:

```
template<int val> class SwitchTemplate
```

The preceding initialization template will also be used for the default value. Next, we will add two templates for each possible value as follows:

```
template<> class SwitchTemplate<1>
template<> class SwitchTemplate<2>
```

Each preceding template will run the `Square()` function and pass the argument based on the value of the template. The complete code is written as follows:

```cpp
/* switchmeta.cpp */
#include <iostream>

using namespace std;

// Function to find out
// the square of an int
int Square(int a)
{
   return a * a;
}

// Defining template for
// default output
// for any input value
template<int val>
class SwitchTemplate
{
  public:
    static inline int func()
    {
       return Square(0);
    }
};

// Defining template for
// specific input value
// 'val' = 1
template<>
class SwitchTemplate<1>
{
    public:
      static inline int func()
```

```
      {
          return Square(1);
      }
};

// Defining template for
// specific input value
// 'val' = 2
template<>
class SwitchTemplate<2>
{
    public:
      static inline int func()
      {
          return Square(2);
      }
};

auto main() -> int
{
    cout << "[switchmeta.cpp]" << endl;

    // Defining a constant variable
    const int i = 2;

    // Consuming the SwitchTemplate template
    int output = SwitchTemplate<i>::func();

    // Displaying the result
    cout << "The result is " << output << endl;

    return 0;
}
```

As we can see, we do the same as `conditionmeta.cpp`--we call the `func()` method inside the template to run the selected function. The value for this `switch-case` condition is the template we put in the angle bracket. If we run the preceding `switchmeta.cpp` code, we will see the following output on the console:

As we can see in the preceding screenshot, we've got the exact same output for `switchmeta.cpp` code as compared to the `switch.cpp` code. Thus, we have successfully refactored the `switch.cpp` code into the template metaprogramming.

Looping the process

We usually use the `do-while` loop when we iterate something. Let's suppose we need to print certain numbers until it reaches zero (0). The code is as follows:

```cpp
/* loop.cpp */
#include <iostream>

using namespace std;

// Function for printing
// given number
void PrintNumber(int i)
{
  cout << i << "\t";
}

auto main() -> int
{
  cout << "[loop.cpp]" << endl;

  // Initializing an int variable
  // marking as maximum number
  int i = 100;

  // Looping to print out
  // the numbers below i variable
  cout << "List of numbers between 100 and 1";
  cout << endl;
  do
  {
    PrintNumber(i);
  }
  while (--i > 0);
  cout << endl;

  return 0;
}
```

As we can see in the preceding code, we will print the number `100`, decrease its value, and print again. It will always run until the number reaches zero (`0`). The output on the console should be as follows:

Now, let's refactor it to the template metaprogramming. Here, we need only two templates to achieve the `do-while` loop in template metaprogramming. First, we will create the following template:

```
template<int limit> class DoWhile
```

The limit in the preceding code is the value that is passed to the `do-while` loop. And, to not make the loop become an infinite loop, we have to design the `DoWhile` template when it has reached zero (`0`), as shown here:

```
template<> class DoWhile<0>
```

The preceding template will do nothing since it's used only to break the loop. The complete refactoring of the `do-while` loop is like the following `loopmeta.cpp` code:

```cpp
/* loopmeta.cpp */
#include <iostream>

using namespace std;

// Function for printing
// given number
void PrintNumber(int i)
{
  cout << i << "\t";
}
```

```cpp
// Defining template for printing number
// passing to its 'limit' parameter
// It's only run
// if the 'limit' has not been reached
template<int limit>
class DoWhile
{
    private:
      enum
      {
        run = (limit-1) != 0
      };

    public:
      static inline void func()
      {
        PrintNumber(limit);
        DoWhile<run == true ? (limit-1) : 0>
          ::func();
      }
};

// Defining template for doing nothing
// when the 'limit' reaches 0
template<>
class DoWhile<0>
{
  public:
    static inline void func()
      {
      }
};

auto main() -> int
{
  cout << "[loopmeta.cpp]" << endl;

  // Defining a constant variable
  const int i = 100;

  // Looping to print out
  // the numbers below i variable
  // by consuming the DoWhile
  cout << "List of numbers between 100 and 1";
  cout << endl;
  DoWhile<i>::func();
  cout << endl;
```

```
        return 0;
    }
```

We then call the `func()` method inside the template to run our desired function. And, if we run the code, we will see the following output on the screen:

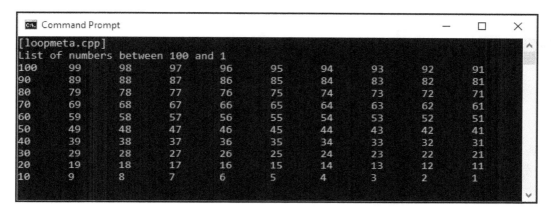

Again, we have successfully refactored the `loop.cpp` code into `loopmeta.cpp` code since both have the exact same output.

Executing the code in compile-time

As we discussed earlier, template metaprogramming will run the code in compile-time by creating a new code. Now, let's see how we can get the compile-time constant and generate a compile-time class in this section.

Getting a compile-time constant

To retrieve a compile-time constant, let's create a code that has the template for a Fibonacci algorithm in it. We will consume the template so the compiler will provide the value in compile time. The code should be as follows:

```cpp
/* fibonaccimeta.cpp */
#include <iostream>

using namespace std;

// Defining Fibonacci template
// to calculate the Fibonacci sequence
```

```cpp
template <int number>
struct Fibonacci
{
  enum
  {
    value =
        Fibonacci<number - 1>::value +
        Fibonacci<number - 2>::value
  };
};

// Defining template for
// specific input value
// 'number' = 1
template <>
struct Fibonacci<1>
{
  enum
  {
    value = 1
  };
};

// Defining template for
// specific input value
// 'number' = 0
template <>
struct Fibonacci<0>
{
  enum
  {
    value = 0
  };
};

auto main() -> int
{
  cout << "[fibonaccimeta.cpp]" << endl;

  // Displaying the compile-time constant
  cout << "Getting compile-time constant:";
  cout << endl;
  cout << "Fibonacci(25) = ";
  cout << Fibonacci<25>::value;
  cout << endl;

  return 0;
}
```

As we can see in the preceding code, the value variable in the Fibonacci template will provide a compile-time constant. And if we run the preceding code, we will see the following output on the console screen:

```
Command Prompt                                          —    □    ×

[fibonaccimeta.cpp]
Getting compile-time constant:
Fibonacci(25) = 75025
```

Now, we have `75025` that is generated by the compiler as a compile-time constant.

Generating the class using a compile-time class generation

Besides the generation of a compile-time constant, we will also generate the class in compile time. Let's suppose we have a template to find out the prime number in the range 0 to X. The following `isprimemeta.cpp` code will explain the implementation of the template metaprogramming to find the prime number:

```cpp
/* isprimemeta.cpp */
#include <iostream>

using namespace std;

// Defining template that decide
// whether or not the passed argument
// is a prime number
template <
  int lastNumber,
  int secondLastNumber>
class IsPrime
{
  public:
    enum
    {
      primeNumber = (
        (lastNumber % secondLastNumber) &&
        IsPrime<lastNumber, secondLastNumber - 1>
            ::primeNumber)
    };
};
```

```cpp
// Defining template for checking
// the number passed to the 'number' parameter
// is a prime number
template <int number>
class IsPrime<number, 1>
{
  public:
    enum
    {
      primeNumber = 1
    };
};

// Defining template to print out
// the passed argument is it's a prime number
template <int number>
class PrimeNumberPrinter
{
  public:
    PrimeNumberPrinter<number - 1> printer;

  enum
  {
    primeNumber = IsPrime<number, number - 1>
        ::primeNumber
  };

  void func()
  {
    printer.func();

    if (primeNumber)
    {
        cout << number << "\t";
    }
  }
};

// Defining template to just ignoring the number
// we pass 1 as argument to the parameter
// since 1 is not prime number
template<>
class PrimeNumberPrinter<1>
{
  public:
    enum
    {
      primeNumber = 0
```

```
        };

        void func()
        {
        }
    };

    int main()
    {
      cout << "[isprimemeta.cpp]" << endl;

      // Displaying the prime numbers between 1 and 500
      cout << "Filtering the numbers between 1 and 500 ";
      cout << "for of the prime numbers:" << endl;

      // Consuming PrimeNumberPrinter template
      PrimeNumberPrinter<500> printer;

      // invoking func() method from the template
      printer.func();

      cout << endl;
      return 0;
    }
```

There are two kinds of templates with different roles--the **prime checker**, that ensures the number that is passed is a prime number, and the **printer**, that displays the prime number to the console. The compiler then generates the class in compile-time when the code accesses `PrimeNumberPrinter<500> printer` and `printer.func()`. And when we run the preceding `isprimemeta.cpp` code, we will see the following output on the console screen:

```
Command Prompt                                                     —    □    ✕
[isprimemeta.cpp]
Filtering the numbers between 1 and 500 for of the prime numbers:
2        3        5        7        11       13       17       19       23       29
31       37       41       43       47       53       59       61       67       71
73       79       83       89       97       101      103      107      109      113
127      131      137      139      149      151      157      163      167      173
179      181      191      193      197      199      211      223      227      229
233      239      241      251      257      263      269      271      277      281
283      293      307      311      313      317      331      337      347      349
353      359      367      373      379      383      389      397      401      409
419      421      431      433      439      443      449      457      461      463
467      479      487      491      499
```

Since we pass 500 to the template, we will get the prime number from 0 to 500. The preceding output has proven that the compiler has successfully generated a compile-time class so we can get the correct value.

Benefits and drawbacks of metaprogramming

After our discussion about template metaprogramming, the following are the advantages we derive:

- Template metaprogramming has no side effect since it is immutable, so we cannot modify an existing type
- There is better code readability compared to code that does not implement metaprogramming
- It reduces repetition of the code

Although we can gain benefits from template metaprogramming, there are several disadvantages, which are as follows:

- The syntax is quite complex.
- The compilation time takes longer since we now execute code during compile-time.
- The compiler can optimize the generated code much better and perform inlining, for instance, the C qsort() function and the C++ sort template. In C, the qsort() function takes a pointer to a comparison function, so there will be one copy of the qsort code that is not inlined. It will make a call through the pointer to the comparison routine. In C++, std::sort is a template, and it can take a functor object as a comparator. There is a different copy of std::sort for each different type used as a comparator. If we use a functor class with an overloaded operator() function, the call to the comparator can easily be inlined into this copy of std::sort.

Summary

Metaprogramming, especially template metaprogramming, creates new code for us automatically so we don't need to write a lot of code in our source. By using template metaprogramming, we can refactor the flow control of our code as well as run the code in compile-time execution.

In the next chapter, we will talk about concurrency techniques that will bring a responsive enhancement to the application that we build. We can run the processes in our code simultaneously using the parallelism technique.

7
Running Parallel Execution Using Concurrency

In the previous chapter, we discussed template metaprogramming that will make a code in compile-time execution. It will also improve the flow control of our code since we can refactor the flow using the template. Now, in this chapter, we will talk about concurrency in C++, where we have to control the flow again when we run two or more processes simultaneously. In this chapter, we will discuss the following topics:

- Running single as well as multiple threads in C++ programming
- Synchronizing the thread to avoid a deadlock
- Using the **handle** resource in Windows to create a thread

Concurrency in C++

Many programming languages have provided support for concurrency today. Instead of sequentially, the computation of the code is executed during overlapping time periods in concurrent programming. It will make our program responsive since the code doesn't need to wait until all computation is finished. Let's suppose we want to develop a program that can play a video and download a huge video file at the same time. Without the concurrency technique, we have to wait for the video to be downloaded successfully before we can play another video file. By using this technique, we can split these two tasks, playing and downloading a video, then run them together concurrently.

Before C++11 was announced, the C++ programmer depended on `Boost::thread` to create a concurrent program using the multithreading technique. In multithreading, we split up the process into the smallest sequence and run these small processes concurrently. Now, in the C++11 library, we get the `thread` class to address our need for concurrency using the multithreading technique.

Processing a single threading code

To use the `thread` class, we just need to create an instance of `std::thread` and pass the function name as the argument. We then call `std::join()` to pause the process until the selected thread finishes its process. Let's take a look at the following `singlethread.cpp` code:

```cpp
/* singlethread.cpp */
#include <thread>
#include <iostream>

using namespace std;

void threadProc()
{
  cout << "Thread ID: ";
  cout << this_thread::get_id() << endl;
}

auto main() -> int
{
  cout << "[singlethread.cpp]" << endl;

  thread thread1(threadProc);
  thread1.join();

  return 0;
}
```

As we can see in the preceding code, we have a function named `threadProc()`, and we pass it into the `thread1` initialization in the `main()` function. After initialization, we call the `join()` method to execute the `thread1` object. The output that we will see on the console should be as follows:

We have successfully run a thread in our code. Now, let's add a piece of code in the `main()` function that will iterate a line of code. We will run them together concurrently. The code for `singlethread2.cpp` is as follows:

```
/* singlethread2.cpp */
#include <thread>
#include <chrono>
#include <iostream>

using namespace std;

void threadProc()
{
  for (int i = 0; i < 5; i++)
  {
    cout << "thread: current i = ";
    cout << i << endl;
  }
}

auto main() -> int
{
  cout << "[singlethread2.cpp]" << endl;

  thread thread1(threadProc);

  for (int i = 0; i < 5; i++)
  {
    cout << "main : current i = " << i << endl;

    this_thread::sleep_for(
        chrono::milliseconds(5));
  }

  thread1.join();

  return 0;
}
```

As we can see in the preceding code, we add a `for` loop to iterate some code and to run it concurrently with `thread1`. To make sense of it, we add a `for` loop in the `threadProc()` function as well. Let's take a look at the following screenshot to figure out what output we will get:

```
C:\WINDOWS\system32\cmd.exe                              —    □    ×

[singlethread2.cpp]
main   : current i = 0
thread: current i = 0
thread: current i = 1
main   : current i = 1
thread: current i = 2
thread: current i = 3
main   : current i = 2
thread: current i = 4
main   : current i = 3
main   : current i = 4
```

We see that the `threadProc()` function and the code in the `main()` function is run together concurrently. Some of you may get a different result, but it's okay since the result cannot be predicted because it depends on the device itself. However, for now, we have been able to run two processes concurrently.

I ran the preceding code multiple times to get the output we see in the preceding screenshot. You might see different order in between the `threadProc()` and `main()` function or get a messy output since the flow of the thread is unpredictable.

Processing a multithreading code

In the multithread technique, we run two or more threads concurrently. Let's suppose we are running five threads simultaneously. We can use the following `multithread.cpp` code that will store these five threads in an array:

```cpp
/* multithread.cpp */
#include <thread>
#include <iostream>

using namespace std;

void threadProc()
{
```

```
    cout << "Thread ID: ";
    cout << this_thread::get_id() << endl;
}

auto main() -> int
{
    cout << "[multithread.cpp]" << endl;

    thread threads[5];

    for (int i = 0; i < 5; ++i)
    {
        threads[i] = thread(threadProc);
    }

    for (auto& thread : threads)
    {
        thread.join();
    }

    return 0;
}
```

After we initialize these five threads based on the preceding code, we will run the `join()` method for all threads to execute them. By using the `join()` method, the program will wait for all processes in the calling threads to be finished, then continue the next process if any. The result we see in the console is as follows:

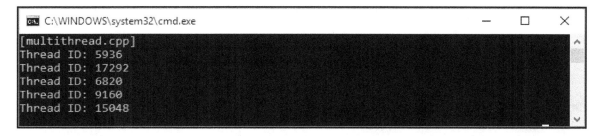

In the preceding screenshot, we see that all five threads have been successfully executed. We can also initialize the thread using the Lambda expression. The following `lambdathread.cpp` code is refactored from the preceding code which uses Lambda instead of creating a separated function:

```
/* lambdathread.cpp */
#include <thread>
#include <iostream>
```

```cpp
using namespace std;

auto main() -> int
{
    cout << "[lambdathread.cpp]" << endl;

    thread threads[5];

    for (int i = 0; i < 5; ++i)
    {
        threads[i] = thread([]()
        {
            cout << "Thread ID: ";
            cout << this_thread::get_id() << endl;
        });
    }

    for (auto& thread : threads)
    {
        thread.join();
    }

    return 0;
}
```

There is no significant change if we see the `lambdathread.cpp` code comparing with the `multithread.cpp` code. However, since the function will only be called once, it's better to use Lambda so it is easier to maintain it. The output we will see on the console is like the following screenshot, not much different compared to the `multithread.cpp` code output:

Although we retrieve the same output when running `lambdathread.cpp` comparing with the `multithread.cpp` code, we have a clear code when we initialize the thread using the Lambda expression. We don't need to create another method to be passed to `Thread`, for instance, `threadProc()`, since this method is actually used only once.

Again, note that the result you see on your screen might be different from the screenshot I gave.

Synchronizing the threads using mutex

As of now, we have successfully executed a multithreading code. However, a problem will occur if we consume a shared object and manipulate it inside the thread. It is called **synchronization**. In this section, we will try to avoid this problem by applying a `mutex` technique.

Avoiding synchronization issues

As we discussed earlier, in this section, we have to ensure that the shared object we run in the thread gives the correct value when it is executing. Let's suppose we have a global variable named `counter` and we plan to increase its value in all the five threads we have. Each thread will execute `10000` times increment iteration, so we expect to get `50000` as a result for all five threads. The code is as follows:

```cpp
/* notsync.cpp */
#include <thread>
#include <iostream>

using namespace std;

auto main() -> int
{
  cout << "[notsync.cpp]" << endl;

  int counter = 0;

  thread threads[5];

  for (int i = 0; i < 5; ++i)
  {
    threads[i] = thread([&counter]()
    {
        for (int i = 0; i < 10000; ++i)
        {
            ++counter;
            cout << "Thread ID: ";
```

```
                    cout << this_thread::get_id();
                    cout << "\tCurrent Counter = ";
                    cout << counter << endl;
            }
    });
}

for (auto& thread : threads)
{
    thread.join();
}

cout << "Final result = " << counter << endl;

return 0;
}
```

Now, let's take a look at the following screenshot we may get on the console when we run the preceding code:

```
C:\Windows\system32\cmd.exe                                 —    □    ×
Thread ID: 8572 Current Counter = 49984
Thread ID: 8572 Current Counter = 49985
Thread ID: 8572 Current Counter = 49986
Thread ID: 8572 Current Counter = 49987
Thread ID: 8572 Current Counter = 49988
Thread ID: 8572 Current Counter = 49989
Thread ID: 8572 Current Counter = 49990
Thread ID: 8572 Current Counter = 49991
Thread ID: 8572 Current Counter = 49992
Thread ID: 8572 Current Counter = 49993
Thread ID: 8572 Current Counter = 49994
Thread ID: 8572 Current Counter = 49995
Final result = 49995
```

Unfortunately, based on the preceding screenshot, we don't get what we expect. This happens because an incrementation process is not an atomic operation since the atomic operation will guarantee the isolation of the concurrent process.

 If you get a different output, don't worry, we are still on the right track as this program demonstrates synchronization issues, as you will see next.

If we trace the output deeper, we will see that there are two threads that execute exactly the same value for the `counter` variable, as we can see in the following screenshot:

We see that the thread with ID `2504` and `5524` access the counter variable when its value is `44143`. That's why we retrieve an unexpected result when we run the preceding code. Now we need to make the increment operation to become an atomic operation that will be executed without any other processes being able to read or change the state that is read or changed during the operation.

To solve this problem, we can use the `mutex` class to make our counter variable `thread-safe`. It means that before the thread accesses the counter variable, it has to ensure that the variable is not accessed by others threads. We can use the `lock()` and `unlock()` methods in the `mutex` class to lock and unlock the targeted variable. Let's take a look at the following `mutex.cpp` code to demonstrate `mutex` implementation:

```cpp
/* mutex.cpp */
#include <thread>
#include <mutex>
#include <iostream>

using namespace std;

auto main() -> int
{
    cout << "[mutex.cpp]" << endl;

    mutex mtx;
    int counter = 0;

    thread threads[5];

    for (int i = 0; i < 5; ++i)
    {
        threads[i] = thread([&counter, &mtx]()
        {
            for (int i = 0; i < 10000; ++i)
```

```
        {
          mtx.lock();
          ++counter;
          mtx.unlock();

          cout << "Thread ID: ";
          cout << this_thread::get_id();
          cout << "\tCurrent Counter = ";
          cout << counter << endl;
        }
    });
  }

  for (auto& thread : threads)
  {
    thread.join();
  }

  cout << "Final result = " << counter << endl;

  return 0;
}
```

As we can see in the preceding code, before the code increments the counter variable, it calls the lock() method. And after that, it calls the unlock() method to notify the other threads that the counter variable is free to manipulate now. If we run the preceding code, we should see the following output on the console:

```
C:\Windows\system32\cmd.exe                            —    □    ×

Thread ID: 6568 Current Counter = 49992
Thread ID: 6568 Current Counter = 49993
Thread ID: 6568 Current Counter = 49994
Thread ID: 6568 Current Counter = 49995
Thread ID: 6568 Current Counter = 49996
Thread ID: 6568 Current Counter = 49997
Thread ID: 6568 Current Counter = 49998
Thread ID: 6568 Current Counter = 49999
Thread ID: 6568 Current Counter = 50000
Final result = 50000
```

By using the mutex class, now we retrieve the result we expect, as we can see in the preceding screenshot.

Unlocking the variable automatically

We now know how to lock the variable to ensure that no two threads working on the same value simultaneously retrieve the correct value from it. However, the problem will occur if an exception is thrown before the thread calls the `unlock()` method. The program will be completely locked if the state of the variable remains locked. To solve this problem, we can use `lock_guard<mutex>` to lock the variable and to ensure that it will be unlocked at the end of the scope no matter what happens. The following piece of code is refactored from the preceding code by adding the `lock_guard<mutex>` functionality:

```cpp
/* automutex.cpp */
#include <thread>
#include <mutex>
#include <iostream>

using namespace std;

auto main() -> int
{
    cout << "[automutex.cpp]" << endl;

    mutex mtx;
    int counter = 0;

    thread threads[5];

    for (int i = 0; i < 5; ++i)
    {
        threads[i] = thread([&counter, &mtx]()
        {
            for (int i = 0; i < 10000; ++i)
            {
                {
                    lock_guard <mutex> guard(mtx);
                    ++counter;
                }

                cout << "Thread ID: ";
                cout << this_thread::get_id();
                cout << "\tCurrent Counter = ";
                cout << counter << endl;
            }
        });
    }

    for (auto& thread : threads)
    {
```

```
        thread.join();
    }

    cout << "Final result = " << counter << endl;

    return 0;
}
```

As we can see from the preceding `automutex.cpp` code, it calls `lock_guard <mutex> guard(mtx)` before it increments the `counter` variable. If we run the code, we will get exactly the same output with the `mutex.cpp` code. However, now we have a program that won't be locked unpredictably.

Avoiding deadlock using recursive mutex

In the previous section, we used `lock_guard` to ensure that the variable is not accessed by more than one thread. However, we will still face a problem if more than one `lock_guard` obtains the lock. In the following piece of code, we have two functions that will call `lock_guard--Multiplexer()` and `Divisor()`. Besides them, we also have a function that will call these two functions--`RunAll()` that will call `lock_guard` first before calling the two functions. The code should look like this:

```
/* deadlock.cpp */
#include <thread>
#include <mutex>
#include <iostream>

using namespace std;

struct Math
{
  mutex mtx;
  int m_content;

  Math() : m_content(0)
  {
  }

  // This method will lock the mutex
  void Multiplexer(int i)
  {
    lock_guard<mutex> lock(mtx);
    m_content *= i;
    cout << "Multiplexer() is called. m_content = ";
    cout << m_content << endl;
```

```
    }

    // This method will lock the mutex also
    void Divisor(int i)
    {
      lock_guard<mutex> lock(mtx);
      m_content /= i;
      cout << "Divisor() is called. m_content = ";
      cout << m_content << endl;
    }

    // This method will invoke
    // the two preceding methods
    // which each method locks the mutex
    void RunAll(int a)
    {
      lock_guard<mutex> lock(mtx);
      Multiplexer(a);
      Divisor(a);
    }
};

auto main() -> int
{
  cout << "[deadlock.cpp]" << endl;

  // Instantiating Math struct
  // and invoking the RunAll() method
  Math math;
  math.RunAll(10);

  return 0;
}
```

We will successfully compile the following piece of code. However, if we run the preceding code, an error will occur since the program won't exit due to the **deadlock**. It is because the same mutex cannot be acquired by multiple threads twice. When the RunAll() function is invoked, it acquires the lock object. The Multiplexer() function inside the RunAll() function wants to acquire lock as well. However, lock has been locked by the RunAll() function. To solve this problem, we can replace lock_guard<mutex> with lock_guard<recursive_mutex>, as you can see in the following piece of code:

```
/* recursivemutex.cpp */
#include <thread>
#include <mutex>
#include <iostream>
```

```cpp
using namespace std;

struct Math
{
  recursive_mutex mtx;
  int m_content;

  Math() : m_content(1)
  {
  }

  // This method will lock the mutex
  void Multiplexer(int i)
  {
    lock_guard<recursive_mutex> lock(mtx);
    m_content *= i;
    cout << "Multiplexer() is called. m_content = ";
    cout << m_content << endl;
  }

  // This method will lock the mutex also
  void Divisor(int i)
  {
    lock_guard<recursive_mutex> lock(mtx);
    m_content /= i;
    cout << "Divisor() is called. m_content = ";
    cout << m_content << endl;
  }

  // This method will invoke
  // the two preceding methods
  // which each method locks the mutex
  void RunAll(int a)
  {
    lock_guard<recursive_mutex> lock(mtx);
    Multiplexer(a);
    Divisor(a);
  }
};

auto main() -> int
{
  cout << "[recursivemutex.cpp]" << endl;

  // Instantiating Math struct
  // and invoking the RunAll() method
  Math math;
  math.RunAll(10);
```

```
    return 0;
  }
```

Now, we can successfully compile and run the preceding code. We can use the `lock_guard<recursive_mutex>` class that will allow mutex to be locked more than once without getting to the deadlock. The following screenshot will be seen on the console when we run the preceding code:

Now, we know we need to use one recursive `mutex` if we want to call functions that lock the same `mutex` recursively.

Understanding the thread processing in a Windows operating system

Let's move to a specific operating system that is widely used by many user computers, that is Windows. Our code must need to be run on some commercial platform from a leading OS vendor, such as Microsoft. So, we will now run the thread in Windows OS. In this OS, the thread is a kernel resource, which means it is an object that is created and owned by the OS kernel and lives in the kernel. The kernel itself is a core program that has complete control over everything in the system. In this section, we will develop a thread in Windows OS so our program can work well in this OS.

Working with handle

In the Windows operating system, handle is an abstract reference value to a resource. In this discussion, we will use the abstract reference to hold the thread. Let's suppose we have a `threadProc()` function that will be called inside a thread which is held in the `hnd` variable. The code will be as follows:

```
/* threadhandle.cpp */
#include <iostream>
#include <windows.h>
```

```
using namespace std;

auto threadProc(void*) -> unsigned long
{
  cout << "threadProc() is run." << endl;
  return 100;
}

auto main() -> int
{
  cout << "[threadhandle.cpp]" << endl;

  auto hnd = HANDLE
  {
    CreateThread(
        nullptr,
        0,
        threadProc,
        nullptr,
        0,
        nullptr)
  };

  if (hnd)
  {
    WaitForSingleObject(hnd, INFINITE);

    unsigned long exitCode;
    GetExitCodeThread(hnd, &exitCode);

    cout << "The result = " << exitCode << endl;

    CloseHandle(hnd);
  }

  return 0;
}
```

As we can see in the preceding code, we use the CreateThread() function provided by the windows.h header to generate a thread. For now, we just pass the nullptr value as the default parameter, except threadProc as a function that we will call from the thread.

After we initialize the handle of the thread, we can ensure that the hnd variable contains the handle of the thread, then invokes the WaitForSingleObject() function. It is similar to the join() method we used in the preceding section that will run the thread and wait until the thread is finished. Since the thread handle is a resource we use, don't forget to release it by using the CloseHandle() function. If we run the preceding code, we will see the following output on the console screen:

As we can see, we have successfully run the thread since we've got the expected process from the threadProc() function.

Refactoring to a unique handle

Now, to ease our programming process, we will create a class named NullHandle that will automatically release the resource each time we no longer need it. It will be constructed from the UniqueHandle class, which we will develop as well. These classes can be found in the uniquehandle.h file. The implementation of UniqueHandle is as follows:

```
template <typename C>
class UniqueHandle
{
  private:
    HANDLE m_val;

    void Close()
    {
      if (*this)
      {
        C::Exit(m_val);
      }
    }

  public:
    // Copy assignment operator
    UniqueHandle(UniqueHandle const &) = delete;
    auto operator=(UniqueHandle const &)->UniqueHandle & = delete;

    // UniqueHandle constructor
```

```cpp
    explicit UniqueHandle(HANDLE value = C::Invalid()) :
    m_val{ value }
    {
    }

    // Move assignment operator
    UniqueHandle(UniqueHandle && other) :
    m_val{ other.Release() }
    {
    }

    // Move assignment operator
    auto operator=(UniqueHandle && other) -> UniqueHandle &
    {
      if (this != &other)
      {
        Reset(other.Release());
      }

      return *this;
    }

    // Destructor of UniqueHandle class
    ~UniqueHandle()
    {
      Close();
    }

    // bool operator for equality
    explicit operator bool() const
    {
      return m_val != C::Invalid();
    }

    // Method for retrieving the HANDLE value
    HANDLE Get() const
    {
      return m_val;
    }

    // Method for releasing the HANDLE value
    HANDLE Release()
    {
      auto value = m_val;
      m_val = C::Invalid();
      return value;
    }
    // Method for reseting the HANDLE
```

```
bool Reset(HANDLE value = C::Invalid())
{
 if (m_val != value)
 {
    Close();
    m_val = value;
 }

  return static_cast<bool>(*this);
}
};
```

As we can see, we have a complete implementation of the UniqueHandle class that can be instanced and will automatically close the handle from its destructor. To use NullHandle object, we will use the following code:

```
using NullHandle = UniqueHandle<NullHandleCharacteristics>;
```

The implementation of the NullHandleCharacteristics struct is as follows:

```
struct NullHandleCharacteristics
{
  // Returning nullptr when the HANDLE is invalid
  static HANDLE Invalid()
  {
     return nullptr;
  }

  // Exit the HANDLE by closing it
  static void Exit(HANDLE val)
  {
     CloseHandle(val);
  }
};
```

Now, let's refactor our preceding threadhandle.cpp code. We will replace HANDLE with NullHandle, so it will be as follows:

```
auto hnd = NullHandle
{
  CreateThread(
    nullptr,
    0,
    threadProc,
    nullptr,
    0,
    nullptr)
};
```

Then, we will create a new function named `WaitOneThread()` to call the thread itself and wait until it finishes. The implementation should be as follows:

```
auto WaitOneThread(
   HANDLE const h,
   DWORD const ms = INFINITE) -> bool
   {
     auto const r = WaitForSingleObject(
     h,
     ms);

     // Inform that thread is not idle
     if (r == WAIT_OBJECT_0)
       return true;

     // Inform that thread is not idle
     if (r == WAIT_TIMEOUT)
       return false;

     throw WinException();
   }
```

By using the `WaitOneThread()` function, we can know whether or not the thread has been run. The `WinException` struct can be implemented as follows:

```
struct WinException
{
  unsigned long error;

  explicit WinException(
    unsigned long value = GetLastError()) :
    error{ value }
    {
    }
};
```

Now, we can add the following piece of code to the `main()` function after we initialize the hnd HANDLE:

```
if (hnd)
{
  if (WaitOneThread(hnd.Get(), 0))
    cout << "Before running thread" << endl;

  WaitOneThread(hnd.Get());

  if (WaitOneThread(hnd.Get(), 0))
    cout << "After running thread" << endl;
```

```
    unsigned long exitCode;
    GetExitCodeThread(hnd.Get(), &exitCode);

    cout << "The result = " << exitCode << endl;
}
```

As we can see from the preceding code, we call the `WaitOneThread()` function and pass 0 as the `ms` parameter to find out the status of the `WaitForSingleObject()` function call. We can pass the `INFINITE` value to it to call the thread and wait for it until it finishes. The following is the `threaduniquehandle.cpp` code that is refactored from the `threadhandle.cpp` code and has consumed the `UniqueHandle` class:

```cpp
/* threaduniquehandle.cpp */
#include <iostream>
#include <windows.h>
#include "../uniquehandle_h/uniquehandle.h"

using namespace std;

unsigned long threadProc(void*)
{
  cout << "threadProc() is run." << endl;
  return 100;
}

struct WinException
{
  unsigned long error;
  explicit WinException(
    unsigned long value = GetLastError()) :
    error{ value }
    {
    }
};

auto WaitOneThread(
  HANDLE const h,
  DWORD const ms = INFINITE) -> bool
  {
    auto const r = WaitForSingleObject(
    h,
    ms);

    // Inform that thread is not idle
    if (r == WAIT_OBJECT_0)
      return true;
```

```
    // Inform that thread is not idle
    if (r == WAIT_TIMEOUT)
      return false;

    throw WinException();
  }

auto main() -> int
{
  cout << "[threaduniquehandle.cpp]" << endl;

  auto hnd = NullHandle
  {
    CreateThread(
        nullptr,
        0,
        threadProc,
        nullptr,
        0,
        nullptr)
  };

  if (hnd)
  {
    if (WaitOneThread(hnd.Get(), 0))
      cout << "Before running thread" << endl;

    WaitOneThread(hnd.Get());

    if (WaitOneThread(hnd.Get(), 0))
      cout << "After running thread" << endl;

    unsigned long exitCode;
    GetExitCodeThread(hnd.Get(), &exitCode);

    cout << "The result = " << exitCode << endl;
  }

  return 0;
}
```

The following screenshot is the output we should see on the console screen:

As we can see from the preceding screenshot, we don't have the `Before running thread` line on it. It's because we will get the `WAIT_TIMEOUT` output each time the thread is not called. And still, we have successfully executed the code in the `threadProc()` function.

Triggering an event

After playing with thread in Windows, let's try another concurrency type--`Event`. It is an action that can be triggered by the system. To know further about it, let's take a look at the following code snippet where we create a new class named `Event` that implements `UniqueHandle` as well:

```
class Event
{
  private:
    NullHandle hnd;

  public:
    Event(Event const &) = delete;
    auto operator=(Event const &)->Event & = delete;
    ~Event() = default;

    explicit Event(bool manual) :
     hnd
     {
       CreateEvent(nullptr,
        manual, false, nullptr)
     }
     {
       if (!hnd)
         throw WinException();
     }

    explicit Event(EventType evType) :
     hnd
```

```
    {
      CreateEvent(
       nullptr,
       static_cast<BOOL>(evType),
       false,
       nullptr)
    }
    {
      if (!hnd)
       throw WinException();
    }

    Event(Event && other) throw() :
      hnd
      {
        other.hnd.Release()
      }
      {
      }

    auto operator=(Event && other) throw()->Event &
    {
      hnd = move(other.hnd);
    }

    void Set()
    {
      cout << "The event is set" << endl;
      SetEvent(hnd.Get());
    }

    void Clear()
    {
      cout << "The event is cleared" << endl;
      ResetEvent(hnd.Get());
    }

    auto Wait(
      DWORD const ms = INFINITE) -> bool
      {
        auto const result = WaitForSingleObject(
        hnd.Get(), ms);

        return result == WAIT_OBJECT_0;
      }
};
```

As we can see in the preceding `Event` class implementation, we have the `Set()`, `Clear()`, and `Wait()` methods to set an event, clear an event, and wait for the event to complete respectively. We have two event types, which are automatic reset and manual reset, which are declared as follows:

```
enum class EventType
{
  AutoReset,
  ManualReset
};
```

Now, we will create content in the `main()` function. We will instance the `Event` class first, then we will check the event signaling. If it's not signaled, we will set the event. On the contrary, we will clear the event. The code will be the following `event.cpp` code:

```
/* event.cpp */
#include <iostream>
#include <windows.h>
#include "../uniquehandle_h/uniquehandle.h"

using namespace std;

struct WinException
{
  unsigned long error;

  explicit WinException(
    unsigned long value = GetLastError()) :
    error{ value }
    {
    }
};

enum class EventType
{
  AutoReset,
  ManualReset
};

class Event
{
  private:
    NullHandle hnd;

  public:
    Event(Event const &) = delete;
    auto operator=(Event const &)->Event & = delete;
```

```cpp
    ~Event() = default;

    explicit Event(bool manual) :
     hnd
     {
       CreateEvent(nullptr,
       manual, false, nullptr)
     }
     {
       if (!hnd)
         throw WinException();
     }

    explicit Event(EventType evType) :
     hnd
      {
        CreateEvent(
        nullptr,
        static_cast<BOOL>(evType),
        false,
        nullptr)
      }
      {
        if (!hnd)
          throw WinException();
      }

    Event(Event && other) throw() :
       hnd
       {
         other.hnd.Release()
       }
       {
       }

    auto operator=(Event && other) throw() -> Event &
    {
        hnd = move(other.hnd);
    }

    void Set()
    {
        cout << "The event is set" << endl;
        SetEvent(hnd.Get());
    }

    void Clear()
    {
```

```
        cout << "The event is cleared" << endl;
        ResetEvent(hnd.Get());
  }

  auto Wait(
    DWORD const ms = INFINITE) -> bool
      {
        auto const result = WaitForSingleObject(
          hnd.Get(), ms);
        return result == WAIT_OBJECT_0;
    }
};

  void CheckEventSignaling( bool b)
  {
    if (b)
    {
      cout << "The event is signaled" << endl;
    }
    else
    {
     cout << "The event is not signaled" << endl;
    }
}

auto main() -> int
{
  cout << "[event.cpp]" << endl;

  auto ev = Event{
    EventType::ManualReset };

    CheckEventSignaling(ev.Wait(0));

    ev.Set();

    CheckEventSignaling(ev.Wait(0));

    ev.Clear();

    CheckEventSignaling(ev.Wait(0));

    return 0;
  }
```

As we can see in the preceding code, here is what the code does:

1. It creates the instance of the `Event` class in the `main()` function and manually resets the event.
2. It invokes the `CheckEventSignaling()` function to find out the status of the event by passing the `Wait()` function to the `CheckEventSignaling()` function, which in turn calls the `WaitForSingleObject()` function.
3. It invokes the `Set()` and `Reset()` functions.
4. Now run the preceding `event.cpp` code. You will see the following output on the console:

```
C:\Windows\system32\cmd.exe                    —  □  ×
[event.cpp]
The event is not signaled
The event is set
The event is signaled
The event is cleared
The event is not signaled
```

If we take a look at the preceding screenshot, at first, the initialization of the `Event` class is not signaled. We then set the event, and it is now signaled as the status from the `CheckEventSignaling()` method. Here, we can say that we can check the status of the signaled event by calling the `WaitForSingleObject()` function.

Calling an event from a thread

Now, let's use thread to call the `Event` class. However, before that, we have to be able to wrap more than one thread, call them together, and wait until their processes are finished. The following code block is a `Wrap()` function that will pack the threads:

```cpp
void Wrap(HANDLE *)
{
}

template <typename T, typename... Args>
void Wrap(
  HANDLE * left,
  T const & right,
  Args const & ... args)
  {
    *left = right.Get();
    Wrap(++left, args...);
  }
```

We will call the preceding `Wrap()` function when we join all the threads. So, we will need another function named `WaitAllThreads()`, as we can see in the following piece of code:

```
template <typename... Args>
void WaitAllThreads(Args const & ... args)
{
   HANDLE handles[sizeof...(Args)];

   Wrap(handles, args...);

   WaitForMultipleObjects(
     sizeof...(Args),
     handles,
     true,
     INFINITE);
}
```

Now, we can create our full code that will run the two threads using the following `eventthread.cpp` code:

```
/* eventthread.cpp */
#include <iostream>
#include <windows.h>
#include "../uniquehandle_h/uniquehandle.h"

using namespace std;

void Wrap(HANDLE *)
{
}

template <typename T, typename... Args>
void Wrap(
  HANDLE * left,
  T const & right,
  Args const & ... args)
  {
    *left = right.Get();
    Wrap(++left, args...);
  }

template <typename... Args>
void WaitAllThreads(Args const & ... args)
{
   HANDLE handles[sizeof...(Args)];

   Wrap(handles, args...);
```

```
    WaitForMultipleObjects(
      sizeof...(Args),
      handles,
      true,
      INFINITE);
  }

  auto threadProc(void*) -> unsigned long
  {
    cout << "Thread ID: ";
    cout << GetCurrentThreadId() << endl;
    return 120;
  }

  auto main() -> int
  {
    cout << "[eventthread.cpp]" << endl;

    auto thread1 = NullHandle
    {
      CreateThread(
        nullptr,
        0,
        threadProc,
        nullptr,
        CREATE_SUSPENDED,
        nullptr)
    };

    auto thread2 = NullHandle
    {
      CreateThread(
        nullptr,
        0,
        threadProc,
        nullptr,
        CREATE_SUSPENDED,
        nullptr)
    };

    ResumeThread(thread1.Get());
    ResumeThread(thread2.Get());

    WaitAllThreads(thread1, thread2);

    return 0;
  }
```

Moreover, if we run the preceding `eventthread.cpp` code, we will see the following output on the console screen:

We have successfully triggered an `Event`, so it can be set to become signaled and can be cleared to become unsignaled in the `event.cpp` code. We have also successfully wrapped more than one thread, then called them together in the `eventthread.cpp` code. Now, let's concatenate these two codes so we can access the event from the thread. The code should be like the following `eventthread2.cpp` code:

```cpp
/* eventthread2.cpp */
#include <iostream>
#include <windows.h>
#include "../uniquehandle_h/uniquehandle.h"

using namespace std;

struct WinException
{
  unsigned long error;

  explicit WinException(
    unsigned long value = GetLastError()) :
    error{ value }
    {
    }
};

enum class EventType
{
  AutoReset,
  ManualReset
};

class Event
{
  private:
    NullHandle hnd;

  public:
```

```
Event(Event const &) = delete;
auto operator=(Event const &)->Event & = delete;
~Event() = default;

explicit Event(bool manual) :
  hnd
  {
    CreateEvent(nullptr,
    manual, false, nullptr)
  }
  {
    if (!hnd)
      throw WinException();
  }

explicit Event(EventType evType) :
  hnd
  {
    CreateEvent(
      nullptr,
      static_cast<BOOL>(evType),
      false,
      nullptr)
  }
  {
    if (!hnd)
      throw WinException();
  }

Event(Event && other) throw() :
  hnd
  {
    other.hnd.Release()
  }
  {
  }

auto operator=(Event && other) throw() -> Event &
{
  hnd = move(other.hnd);
}

void Set()
{
  cout << "The event is set" << endl;
  SetEvent(hnd.Get());
}
```

```cpp
    void Clear()
    {
      cout << "The event is cleared" << endl;
      ResetEvent(hnd.Get());
    }

    auto Wait( DWORD const ms = INFINITE) -> bool
    {
        auto const result = WaitForSingleObject(
         hnd.Get(), ms);

        return result == WAIT_OBJECT_0;
    }
};

    void Wrap(HANDLE *)
    {
    }

    template <typename T, typename... Args>
    void Wrap(
    HANDLE * left,
    T const & right,
    Args const & ... args)
    {
      *left = right.Get();
        Wrap(++left, args...);
    }

    template <typename... Args>
    void WaitAllThreads(Args const & ... args)
    {
    HANDLE handles[sizeof...(Args)];

    Wrap(handles, args...);

    WaitForMultipleObjects(
      sizeof...(Args),
      handles,
      true,
      INFINITE);
    }

    static auto ev = Event{
    EventType::ManualReset };

    auto threadProc(void*) -> unsigned long
    {
```

```
        cout << "Thread ID: ";
        cout << GetCurrentThreadId() << endl;

        ev.Wait();

        cout << "Run Thread ID: ";
        cout << GetCurrentThreadId() << endl;

        return 120;
}

auto main() -> int
{
        cout << "[eventthread2.cpp]" << endl;

        auto thread1 = NullHandle
        {
          CreateThread(
            nullptr,
            0,
            threadProc,
            nullptr,
            0,
            nullptr)
        };

        auto thread2 = NullHandle
        {
          CreateThread(
            nullptr,
            0,
            threadProc,
            nullptr,
            0,
            nullptr)
        };

        Sleep(100);
        ev.Set();
        Sleep(100);

        WaitAllThreads(thread1, thread2);

        return 0;
}
```

In the preceding `eventthread2.cpp` code, we try to trigger the event using the thread. We initialize two `NullHandle` object threads at first. Then, we set the event and call the `Sleep()` function to make the event active. The `WaitAllThreads()` function then invokes the `threadProc()` function and runs each thread. This will trigger the event by calling the `ev.Wait()` function. The threads will be run then. The following screenshot is the output we will see on the console screen:

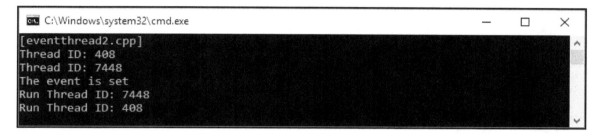

The preceding code is the event that we set manually to reset the event. This means that we have to state when we clear the event. Now, we pass `AutoReset` to the event instance. We will also modify the `threadProc()` function a little bit. The following piece of code is `eventthread3.cpp` that we are talking about:

```cpp
/* eventthread3.cpp */
#include <iostream>
#include <windows.h>
#include "../uniquehandle_h/uniquehandle.h"

using namespace std;

struct WinException
{
  unsigned long error;

  explicit WinException(
    unsigned long value = GetLastError()) :
    error{ value }
    {
    }
};

enum class EventType
{
  AutoReset,
  ManualReset
};
```

```
class Event
{
    private:
      NullHandle hnd;

    public:
      Event(Event const &) = delete;
      auto operator=(Event const &)->Event & = delete;
      ~Event() = default;

      explicit Event(bool manual) :
        hnd
        {
          CreateEvent(nullptr,
          manual, false, nullptr)
        }
        {
          if (!hnd)
            throw WinException();
        }

        explicit Event(EventType evType) :
          hnd
          {
            CreateEvent(
              nullptr,
              static_cast<BOOL>(evType),
              false,
              nullptr)
          }
          {
            if (!hnd)
              throw WinException();
          }

      Event(Event && other) throw() :
        hnd
        {
          other.hnd.Release()
        }
        {
        }

      auto operator=(Event && other) throw() -> Event &
        {
          hnd = move(other.hnd);
        }
```

```cpp
    void Set()
    {
        cout << "The event is set" << endl;
        SetEvent(hnd.Get());
    }

    void Clear()
    {
        cout << "The event is cleared" << endl;
        ResetEvent(hnd.Get());
    }

    auto Wait(
      DWORD const ms = INFINITE) -> bool
      {
        auto const result = WaitForSingleObject(
          hnd.Get(), ms);

       return result == WAIT_OBJECT_0;
      }
};

  void Wrap(HANDLE *)
  {
  }

  template <typename T, typename... Args>
  void Wrap(
    HANDLE * left,
    T const & right,
    Args const & ... args)
    {
      *left = right.Get();
      Wrap(++left, args...);
    }

  template <typename... Args>
  void WaitAllThreads(Args const & ... args)
  {
      HANDLE handles[sizeof...(Args)];

      Wrap(handles, args...);

      WaitForMultipleObjects(
        sizeof...(Args),
        handles,
        true,
        INFINITE);
```

```
}

static auto ev = Event{
EventType::AutoReset };

auto threadProc(void*) -> unsigned long
{
  cout << "Thread ID: ";
  cout << GetCurrentThreadId() << endl;

  ev.Wait();

  cout << "Run Thread ID: ";
  cout << GetCurrentThreadId() << endl;

  Sleep(1000);
  ev.Set();

  return 120;
}

auto main() -> int
{
  cout << "[eventthread3.cpp]" << endl;

  auto thread1 = NullHandle
  {
    CreateThread(
      nullptr,
      0,
      threadProc,
      nullptr,
      0,
      nullptr)
  };

  auto thread2 = NullHandle
  {
    CreateThread(
      nullptr,
      0,
      threadProc,
      nullptr,
      0,
      nullptr)
  };

  Sleep(100);
```

```
        ev.Set();
        Sleep(100);

        WaitAllThreads(thread1, thread2);

        return 0;
    }
```

As we can see in the preceding code, we move the `Set()` method of the event from the `main()` function to the `threadProc()` function. Now, every time the `threadProc()` function is invoked, the event is set automatically. The following screenshot is the output we should see on the console screen:

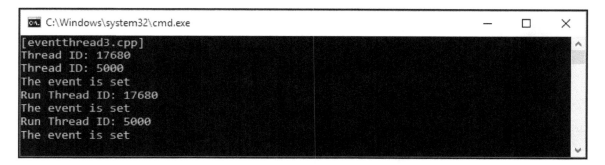

Summary

We have learned a concept of C++ concurrency in this chapter. We now can process a single thread as well as multithreads. We can also synchronize the multithreads so it can run smoothly; therefore, we can avoid synchronization issues and deadlock. Lastly, we can consume the handle resource in Windows to create a thread and trigger the event using that event.

In the next chapter, we will apply all we have learned in the previous chapters to produce an application in a functional way. It will also explain how to test an application that is built using the C++ language.

8
Creating and Debugging Application in Functional Approach

We discussed some basic techniques to develop functional programming in the previous chapters that include a first-class function, a pure function, and an immutable object. In this chapter, we will use all the techniques we have learned in the previous chapters to produce an application in a functional way. It will also explain how to debug an application that is built using the C++ language.

In this chapter, we will cover the following topics:

- Preparing an imperative code as a base code to be transformed to the functional code
- Implementing the pure function to the base code
- Implementing the template metaprogramming to the base code
- Implementing the filtering technique to the base code using the Lambda expression
- Implementing the recursion technique to the base code
- Implementing the memoization technique to the base code
- Debugging the code to solve, if we get an unexpected result

Preparing an imperative class

We will now develop the functional class so we can consume it to our functional program. Before that, let's prepare a new imperative class named `Customer`. The class will have an `int` property named `id` as a unique customer ID number. It also has four string properties to store the information about our customer--`name`, `address`, `phoneNumber`, and `email`. The class also has a flag--`isActive`--to indicate whether or not our customer is active. If the customer has signed a contract with us, they are regarded as an active customer. Another property is `registeredCustomers`, to save all registered customers we have, regardless of the active customer. We will make the `registeredCustomers` member become `static` so we can fill it from outside the class and can keep the list of the `Customer` class.

Besides these properties, our class will also have four methods to access the list of our properties. They will be the following methods:

- `GetActiveCustomerNames()`: This can be used to get the list of active customer names
- `GetActiveCustomerAddresses()`: This can be used to get the list of active customer addresses
- `GetActiveCustomerPhoneNumbers()`: This can be used to get the list of active customer phone numbers
- `GetActiveCustomerEmails()`: This can be used to get the list of active customer emails

Now, let's take a look at the following `Customer.h` code that we can find in the `Step01` folder to accommodate our preceding scenario:

```
/* Customer.h - Step01 */
#ifndef __CUSTOMER_H__
#define __CUSTOMER_H__

#include <string>
#include <vector>

class Customer
{
  public:
    static std::vector<Customer> registeredCustomers;
    int id = 0;
    std::string name;
    std::string address;
    std::string phoneNumber;
    std::string email;
```

```
      bool isActive = true;

      std::vector<std::string> GetActiveCustomerNames();
      std::vector<std::string> GetActiveCustomerAddresses();
      std::vector<std::string> GetActiveCustomerPhoneNumbers();
      std::vector<std::string> GetActiveCustomerEmails();
};
#endif // __CUSTOMER_H__
```

From the preceding code, we have four public methods that haven't been defined yet. Now, let's define them as we can see in the following Customer.cpp code:

```
/* Customer.cpp - Step01 */
#include "Customer.h"

using namespace std;

vector<Customer> Customer::registeredCustomers;

vector<string> Customer::GetActiveCustomerNames()
{
  vector<string> returnList;
  for (auto &customer : Customer::registeredCustomers)
  {
    if (customer.isActive)
    {
        returnList.push_back(customer.name);
    }
  }
   return returnList;
}

vector<string> Customer::GetActiveCustomerAddresses()
{
  vector<string> returnList;
  for (auto &customer : Customer::registeredCustomers)
  {
    if (customer.isActive)
    {
        returnList.push_back(customer.address);
    }
  }
  return returnList;
}

vector<string> Customer::GetActiveCustomerPhoneNumbers()
{
  vector<string> returnList;
```

```
      for (auto &customer : Customer::registeredCustomers)
      {
        if (customer.isActive)
        {
            returnList.push_back(customer.phoneNumber);
        }
      }
      return returnList;
}

vector<string> Customer::GetActiveCustomerEmails()
{
    vector<string> returnList;
    for (auto &customer : Customer::registeredCustomers)
    {
        if (customer.isActive)
        {
            returnList.push_back(customer.email);
        }
    }
    return returnList;
}
```

From the preceding code, we can see the definition of the four methods we have in the Customer class. For instance, in the GetActiveCustomerNames() method, the code loops each element in the registeredCustomers vector to find out the active customer. If it finds them, the code will extract the name of each customer and store it to the returnList vector. After finishing the method process, the method will feed the returnList result to the method user.

Now, let's consume the preceding class using the following main.cpp code:

```
/* Main.cpp - Step01 */
#include <iostream>
#include <algorithm>
#include "Customer.h"

using namespace std;

void RegisterCustomers()
{
    int i = 0;
    bool b = false;

    // Initialize name
    vector<string> nameList =
    {
```

```
        "William",
        "Aiden",
        "Rowan",
        "Jamie",
        "Quinn",
        "Haiden",
        "Logan",
        "Emerson",
        "Sherlyn",
        "Molly"
    };

    // Clear the registeredCustomers vector array
    Customer::registeredCustomers.clear();

    for (auto name : nameList)
    {
        // Create Customer object
        // and fill all properties
        Customer c;
        c.id = i++;
        c.name = name;
        c.address = "somewhere";
        c.phoneNumber = "0123";
        c.email = name + "@xyz.com";
        c.isActive = b;

        // Flip the b value
        b = !b;

        // Send data to the registeredCustomers
        Customer::registeredCustomers.push_back(c);
    }
}

auto main() -> int
{
    cout << "[Step01]" << endl;
    cout << "--------" << endl;

    // Fill the Customer::registeredCustomers
    // with the content
    RegisterCustomers();

    // Instance Customer object
    Customer customer;

    // Get the active customer names
```

```
    cout << "List of active customer names:" << endl;
    vector<string> activeCustomerNames =
      customer.GetActiveCustomerNames();
    for (auto &name : activeCustomerNames)
    {
      cout << name << endl;
    }

    return 0;
}
```

From the preceding code, in the `main()` method, we can see that we first register our customer from the `RegisterCustomers()` method. There, we fill the static public property of the `Customer` class, `registeredCustomers`, with a bunch of our customer information. After that, the code instances the `Customer` class and invokes the method of the class named `GetActiveCustomerNames()`. As we can see, the method returns a vector of string that contains the list of active customer names that we will then store in the `activeCustomerNames` vector. Now, we can iterate the vector to extract the list of the active customer names. The following is the output we should see in the console:

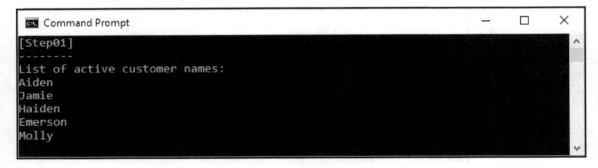

As we can see in the `RegisterCustomer()` method, only five from ten customers are active, so not all of the names will be listed in the preceding output. We can try the remaining three methods to the information about the active customers specifically, their addresses, phone numbers, and email addresses. Our goal in this chapter is to use the concepts we've learned in the previous chapters and make an application using the functional approach. So, let's see how we can achieve that.

Refactoring the imperative class to become a functional class

Indeed, the preceding `Customer` class can work well, and we have successfully invoked its methods. However, the class can still be tweaked by transforming it into a functional class. As we can see in the preceding code, we can implement a pure function, first-class function, higher-order function, and memoization to it to make it become functional. So, in this section, we will refactor the `Customer` class to become a functional class and use the knowledge we have from the previous chapters. In the upcoming section, we will implement the functional method that we have discussed in the previous chapter, which is the first-class function.

Passing a function as a parameter

As we discussed in `Chapter 2`, *Manipulating Functions in Functional Programming*, we can rewrite the function to be a first-class function, which means we can pass a function to another function. We will simplify the definition of all the four methods we have in the `Step01` code, then we will call the function by passing it to another method named `GetActiveCustomerByFunctionField()`. We will also create a new method named `GetActiveCustomerByField()` to select the correct method we should run. The definition of the `Customer` class is now like the following `Customer.h` code:

```
/* Customer.h - Step02 */
#ifndef __CUSTOMER_H__
#define __CUSTOMER_H__

#include <string>
#include <vector>
#include <functional>

class Customer
{
  private:
    std::string GetActiveCustomerNames(
      Customer customer) const;
    std::string GetActiveCustomerAddresses(
      Customer customer) const;
    std::string GetActiveCustomerPhoneNumbers(
      Customer customer) const;
    std::string GetActiveCustomerEmails(
      Customer customer) const;
```

```
    public:
        static std::vector<Customer> registeredCustomers;
        int id = 0;
        std::string name;
        std::string address;
        std::string phoneNumber;
        std::string email;
        bool isActive = true;

        std::vector<std::string> GetActiveCustomerByField(
            const std::string &field);

        std::vector<std::string> GetActiveCustomerByFunctionField(
            std::function<std::string(const Customer&, Customer)>
            funcField);
};
#endif //#ifndef __CUSTOMER_H__
```

As we can see in the preceding header file, besides the four private methods, we add a new public method named GetActiveCustomerByFunctionField(), which we will invoke when we need a list of one of the properties. Now, let's define the four methods we create in the preceding header file. The code should be as the following Customer.cpp file:

```
/* Customer.cpp - Step02 */
#include <stdexcept>
#include "Customer.h"

using namespace std;

vector<Customer> Customer::registeredCustomers;

string Customer::GetActiveCustomerNames(
    Customer customer) const
    {
        return customer.name;
    }

string Customer::GetActiveCustomerAddresses(
    Customer customer) const
    {
        return customer.address;
    }

string Customer::GetActiveCustomerPhoneNumbers(
    Customer customer) const
    {
        return customer.phoneNumber;
    }
```

```
string Customer::GetActiveCustomerEmails(
  Customer customer) const
  {
    return customer.email;
  }

vector<string> Customer::GetActiveCustomerByFunctionField(
  function<string(const Customer&, Customer)> funcField)
  {
    vector<string> returnList;

    Customer c;
    for (auto customer : Customer::registeredCustomers)
    {
      if (customer.isActive)
      {
        returnList.push_back(
            funcField(c, customer));
      }
    }
    return returnList;
  }

  vector<string> Customer::GetActiveCustomerByField(
  const string &field)
  {
  function<string(const Customer&, Customer)> funct;

  if (field == "name")
  {
    funct = &Customer::GetActiveCustomerNames;
  }
  else if (field == "address")
  {
    funct = &Customer::GetActiveCustomerAddresses;
  }
  else if (field == "phoneNumber")
  {
    funct = &Customer::GetActiveCustomerPhoneNumbers;
  }
  else if (field == "email")
  {
    funct = &Customer::GetActiveCustomerEmails;
  }
  else
  {
    throw invalid_argument("Unknown field");
  }
```

```
    return GetActiveCustomerByFunctionField(funct);
}
```

Comparing with the `Step01` code, the implementation of the
`GetActiveCustomerNames()`, `GetActiveCustomerAddresses()`,
`GetActiveCustomerPhoneNumbers()`, and `GetActiveCustomerEmails()` methods is
more concise now. They only contain a single line code. However, we need a new method
to accommodate the process to get a list of the class' private properties, that is the
`GetActiveCustomerByField()` method. The method is passed to the function to make it a
first-class function, as we can see in the preceding code. In this `Step02` folder, the
`main.cpp` code should be as follows:

```cpp
/* Main.cpp - Step02 */
#include <iostream>
#include "Customer.h"

using namespace std;

void RegisterCustomers()
{
  int i = 0;
  bool b = false;

  // Initialize name
  vector<string> nameList =
  {
    "William",
    "Aiden",
    "Rowan",
    "Jamie",
    "Quinn",
    "Haiden",
    "Logan",
    "Emerson",
    "Sherlyn",
    "Molly"
  };

  // Clear the registeredCustomers vector array
  Customer::registeredCustomers.clear();
  for (auto name : nameList)
  {
    // Create Customer object
    // and fill all properties
    Customer c;
    c.id = i++;
    c.name = name;
```

```
        c.address = "somewhere";
        c.phoneNumber = "0123";
        c.email = name + "@xyz.com";
        c.isActive = b;

        // Flip the b value
        b = !b;

        // Send data to the registeredCustomers
        Customer::registeredCustomers.push_back(c);
    }
}

auto main() -> int
{
    cout << "[Step02]" << endl;
    cout << "--------" << endl;

    // Fill the Customer::registeredCustomers
    // with the content
    RegisterCustomers();

    // Instance Customer object
    Customer customer;

    // Get the active customer names
    cout << "List of active customer names:" << endl;
    vector<string> activeCustomerNames =
        customer.GetActiveCustomerByField("name");
    for (auto &name : activeCustomerNames)
    {
        cout << name << endl;
    }

    return 0;
}
```

As we can see in the preceding `main.cpp` code, we will now invoke the
`GetActiveCustomerByField()` method instead of `GetActiveCustomerNames()`, as we
do in `Step01`. We just need to pass a field name in string data type to the
`GetActiveCustomerNames()` method and it will call the appropriate method to retrieve
the properties value. For instance, we will retrieve the `name` properties value because we
pass `name` in the `GetActiveCustomerByField()` method. And, if we run the preceding
`Step02` code, we should see the following screenshot, which is exactly the same as what we
see in the `Step01` code:

```
Command Prompt                                    —    □    ×
[Step02]
--------
List of active customer names:
Aiden
Jamie
Haiden
Emerson
Molly
```

Although we have the code running properly, there's a problem we will face if we want to add more fields or properties to the class, and then need to collect the list of that new field. By using the preceding code, we have to add a new `else` section in the `GetActiveCustomerByFunctionField()` method. Next, we will find the solution to counter it.

Adding a base class

If we want to add more fields in the class and want to access the list of it easily every time we add a new field, we have to create a new class that derives from a base class containing a virtual function. By doing this, we can derive the base class virtual method and implement the correct code to it. We will also gain the power of template metaprogramming here, since we will design the base class as a template. The declaration of the base class will be as follows:

```cpp
template<typename T, typename U>
class BaseClass
{
  public:
    virtual U InvokeFunction(
      const std::shared_ptr<T>&) = 0;
};
```

Now, we can declare four new classes derived from the base class for the four methods in the class. The declaration of the classes should be as follows:

```cpp
class CustomerName :
  public BaseClass<Customer, std::string>
  {
    public:
      virtual std::string InvokeFunction(
        const std::shared_ptr<Customer> &customer)
      {
```

```
          return customer->name;
      }
  };

class CustomerAddress :
  public BaseClass<Customer, std::string>
  {
    public:
      virtual std::string InvokeFunction(
        const std::shared_ptr<Customer> &customer)
        {
          return customer->address;
        }
  };

class CustomerPhoneNumber :
  public BaseClass<Customer, std::string>
  {
      public:
        virtual std::string InvokeFunction(
          const std::shared_ptr<Customer> &customer)
          {
            return customer->phoneNumber;
          }
  };

class CustomerEmail :
  public BaseClass<Customer, std::string>
  {
    public:
      virtual std::string InvokeFunction(
        const std::shared_ptr<Customer> &customer)
        {
          return customer->email;
        }
};
```

We also need to modify the argument type for the
`GetActiveCustomerByFunctionField()` method, so the signature of the method should
be as follows:

```
template<typename T>
static std::vector<T> GetActiveCustomerByFunctionField(
  const std::shared_ptr<BaseClass<Customer, T>>
    &classField);
```

Additionally, the complete header file for this `Step03` code that implements the preceding codes should be as follows:

```
/* Customer.h - Step03 */
#ifndef __CUSTOMER_H__
#define __CUSTOMER_H__

#include <string>
#include <vector>
#include <memory>

class Customer
{
  private:
    template<typename T, typename U>
    class BaseClass
    {
      public:
        virtual U InvokeFunction(
        const std::shared_ptr<T>&) = 0;
    };

    class CustomerName :
    public BaseClass<Customer, std::string>
    {
      public:
        virtual std::string InvokeFunction(
          const std::shared_ptr<Customer> &customer)
          {
            return customer->name;
          }
    };

    class CustomerAddress :
    public BaseClass<Customer, std::string>
    {
      public:
        virtual std::string InvokeFunction(
          const std::shared_ptr<Customer> &customer)
          {
            return customer->address;
          }
    };

    class CustomerPhoneNumber :
    public BaseClass<Customer, std::string>
    {
      public:
```

```cpp
      virtual std::string InvokeFunction(
        const std::shared_ptr<Customer> &customer)
        {
          return customer->phoneNumber;
        }
    };

  class CustomerEmail :
    public BaseClass<Customer, std::string>
    {
      public:
        virtual std::string InvokeFunction(
          const std::shared_ptr<Customer> &customer)
          {
            return customer->email;
          }
    };

  public:
    static std::vector<Customer> registeredCustomers;
    int id = 0;
    std::string name;
    std::string address;
    std::string phoneNumber;
    std::string email;
    bool isActive = true;

    static std::vector<std::string> GetActiveCustomerNames();
    static std::vector<std::string>
      GetActiveCustomerAddresses();
    static std::vector<std::string>
      GetActiveCustomerPhoneNumbers();
    static std::vector<std::string> GetActiveCustomerEmails();

    template<typename T>
    static std::vector<T> GetActiveCustomerByFunctionField(
      const std::shared_ptr<BaseClass<Customer, T>>
      &classField);
};
#endif // __CUSTOMER_H__
```

Now, each method in each preceding class has a different task and can be identified by the class' name. We will also modify the `GetActiveCustomerByFunctionField()` method implementation since it's now passed a new argument type, which is the class name. By passing a class, it's now easier to pass our desired task that lied in the class' method. The implementation of the `GetActiveCustomerByFunctionField()` method should be as follows:

```
template<typename T>
vector<T> Customer::GetActiveCustomerByFunctionField(
  const shared_ptr<BaseClass<Customer, T>> &classField)
  {
    vector<T> returnList;
    for (auto customer : Customer::registeredCustomers)
    {
      if (customer.isActive)
        {
         returnList.push_back(
            classField->InvokeFunction(
              make_shared<Customer>(customer)));
        }
    }
    return returnList;
  }
```

As we can see, the preceding method can run the method of the class we have passed, which is `classField`. Moreover, since the class we have is derived from the `BaseClass` class, we can notify the method to receive the parameter typed `BaseClass`.

Now we can implement the public method that we have declared in the header file-- the `GetActiveCustomerNames()`, `GetActiveCustomerAddresses()`, `GetActiveCustomerPhoneNumbers()`, and `GetActiveCustomerEmails()` methods. These four methods will invoke the `GetActiveCustomerByFunctionField()` method and pass the definition of the `InvokeFunction()` method. The code should be as follows:

```
vector<string> Customer::GetActiveCustomerNames()
{
  return Customer::GetActiveCustomerByFunctionField<string>(
    make_shared<CustomerName>());
}

vector<string> Customer::GetActiveCustomerAddresses()
{
  return Customer::GetActiveCustomerByFunctionField<string>(
    make_shared<CustomerAddress>());
}
```

```cpp
vector<string> Customer::GetActiveCustomerPhoneNumbers()
{
  return Customer::GetActiveCustomerByFunctionField<string>(
    make_shared<CustomerPhoneNumber>());
}

vector<string> Customer::GetActiveCustomerEmails()
{
  return Customer::GetActiveCustomerByFunctionField<string>(
    make_shared<CustomerEmail>());
}
```

Then, we will have a complete `Customer.cpp` file as follows:

```cpp
/* Customer.cpp - Step03 */
#include "Customer.h"

using namespace std;

vector<Customer> Customer::registeredCustomers;

vector<string> Customer::GetActiveCustomerNames()
{
  return Customer::GetActiveCustomerByFunctionField<string>(
    make_shared<CustomerName>());
}

vector<string> Customer::GetActiveCustomerAddresses()
{
  return Customer::GetActiveCustomerByFunctionField<string>(
    make_shared<CustomerAddress>());
}

vector<string> Customer::GetActiveCustomerPhoneNumbers()
{
  return Customer::GetActiveCustomerByFunctionField<string>(
    make_shared<CustomerPhoneNumber>());
}

vector<string> Customer::GetActiveCustomerEmails()
{
  return Customer::GetActiveCustomerByFunctionField<string>(
    make_shared<CustomerEmail>());
}

template<typename T>
vector<T> Customer::GetActiveCustomerByFunctionField(
const shared_ptr<BaseClass<Customer, T>> &classField)
```

```
    {
      vector<T> returnList;
      for (auto &customer : Customer::registeredCustomers)
      {
        if (customer.isActive)
        {
          returnList.push_back(
            classField->InvokeFunction(
              make_shared<Customer>(customer)));
        }
      }
      return returnList;
    }
```

By having the `Customer.h` and `Customer.cpp` code in this `Step03` folder, it's now easier for us to fetch the list of the properties we have in the `Customer` class. For instance, if we want to retrieve a list of active customers, we can directly invoke the `GetActiveCustomerNames()` method, as we can see in the following `main.cpp` code:

```
/* Main.cpp - Step03 */
#include <iostream>
#include "Customer.h"

using namespace std;

void RegisterCustomers()
{
  int i = 0;
  bool b = false;

  // Initialize name
  vector<string> nameList =
  {
    "William",
    "Aiden",
    "Rowan",
    "Jamie",
    "Quinn",
    "Haiden",
    "Logan",
    "Emerson",
    "Sherlyn",
    "Molly"
  };

  // Clear the registeredCustomers vector array
  Customer::registeredCustomers.clear();
```

```
    for (auto name : nameList)
    {
      // Create Customer object
      // and fill all properties
      Customer c;
      c.id = i++;
      c.name = name;
      c.address = "somewhere";
      c.phoneNumber = "0123";
      c.email = name + "@xyz.com";
      c.isActive = b;

      // Flip the b value
      b = !b;

      // Send data to the registeredCustomers
      Customer::registeredCustomers.push_back(c);
    }
}

auto main() -> int
{
  cout << "[Step03]" << endl;
  cout << "--------" << endl;

  // Fill the Customer::registeredCustomers
  // with the content
  RegisterCustomers();

  // Instance Customer object
  Customer customer;

  // Get the active customer names
  cout << "List of active customer names:" << endl;
  vector<string> activeCustomerNames =
    customer.GetActiveCustomerNames();
  for (auto &name : activeCustomerNames)
  {
    cout << name << endl;
  }

   return 0;
}
```

Now, let's run the program in the `Step03` folder. We should see the following screenshot on the console:

```
Command Prompt                                       —    □    ×
[Step03]
--------
List of active customer names:
Aiden
Jamie
Haiden
Emerson
Molly
```

Again, we've got the exact same output comparing the previous step. We will make the `Customer` class become pure in the next section. So, keep going!

Transforming the class to become pure

As we discussed in `Chapter 2`, *Manipulating Functions in Functional Programming*, we have to create a pure function in functional programming to avoid the side effect. If we come back to the previous `GetActiveCustomerByFunctionField()` method definition, it iterates a `registeredCustomers` static member that is a global variable. It will be a problem since the `GetActiveCustomerByFunctionField()` method will feed a different output, although with the exact same passed as an argument.

To counter this problem, we have to abolish this global variable. We then have to modify the method definition as follows:

```cpp
template<typename T>
vector<T> Customer::GetActiveCustomerByFunctionField(
  vector<Customer> customers,
  const shared_ptr<BaseClass<Customer, T>>
    &classField)
    {
      vector<T> returnList;
      for (auto &customer : customers)
      {
        if (customer.isActive)
        {
          returnList.push_back(
            classField->InvokeFunction(
            make_shared<Customer>(customer)));
```

```
      }
    }
    return returnList;
  }
```

Since we don't have the `registeredCustomers` properties anymore, we also have to pass a registered customer list to the `GetActiveCustomerByFunctionField()` method. The method will then iterate the customer list we pass, to find the active customer. Moreover, because we have modified the method signature, we also have to modify the method declaration in the `Customer.h` file as follows:

```
template<typename T>
static std::vector<T> GetActiveCustomerByFunctionField(
  std::vector<Customer> customers,
  const std::shared_ptr<BaseClass<Customer, T>>
    &classField);
```

We discussed that the `GetActiveCustomerByFunctionField()` method is called by the other methods in the `Customer` class. As a result, we also have to modify the method implementation, as we can see in the following code snippet:

```
vector<string> Customer::GetActiveCustomerNames(
  vector<Customer> customers)
  {
    return Customer::GetActiveCustomerByFunctionField<string>(
    customers,
    make_shared<CustomerName>());
  }

vector<string> Customer::GetActiveCustomerAddresses(
  vector<Customer> customer)
  {
    return Customer::GetActiveCustomerByFunctionField<string>(
    customer,
    make_shared<CustomerAddress>());
  }

vector<string> Customer::GetActiveCustomerPhoneNumbers(
  vector<Customer> customer)
  {
    return Customer::GetActiveCustomerByFunctionField<string>(
    customer,
    make_shared<CustomerPhoneNumber>());
  }

vector<string> Customer::GetActiveCustomerEmails(
  vector<Customer> customer)
```

```
    {
      return Customer::GetActiveCustomerByFunctionField<string>(
      customer,
      make_shared<CustomerEmail>());
    }
```

We also need to modify the method declarations in the `Customer.h` file, as shown in the following code snippet:

```
static std::vector<std::string> GetActiveCustomerNames(
  std::vector<Customer> customer);
static std::vector<std::string> GetActiveCustomerAddresses(
  std::vector<Customer> customer);
static std::vector<std::string> GetActiveCustomerPhoneNumbers(
  std::vector<Customer> customer);
static std::vector<std::string> GetActiveCustomerEmails(
  std::vector<Customer> customer);
```

Now, the `Customer.h` file will contain the following complete code block:

```
/* Customer.h - Step04 */
#ifndef __CUSTOMER_H__
#define __CUSTOMER_H__

#include <string>
#include <vector>
#include <memory>

class Customer
{
  private:
    template<typename T, typename U>
    class BaseClass
    {
      public:
        virtual U InvokeFunction(
        const std::shared_ptr<T>&) = 0;
    };

    class CustomerName :
      public BaseClass<Customer, std::string>
      {
        public:
          virtual std::string InvokeFunction(
            const std::shared_ptr<Customer> &customer)
            {
              return customer->name;
            }
```

```
      };

   class CustomerAddress :
     public BaseClass<Customer, std::string>
     {
       public:
         virtual std::string InvokeFunction(
           const std::shared_ptr<Customer> &customer)
           {
         return customer->address;
       }
};

  class CustomerPhoneNumber :
    public BaseClass<Customer, std::string>
    {
      public:
        virtual std::string InvokeFunction(
          const std::shared_ptr<Customer> &customer)
          {
            return customer->phoneNumber;
          }
    };

  class CustomerEmail :
    public BaseClass<Customer, std::string>
    {
      public:
        virtual std::string InvokeFunction(
        const std::shared_ptr<Customer> &customer)
        {
          return customer->email;
        }
    };

  public:
    int id = 0;
    std::string name;
    std::string address;
    std::string phoneNumber;
    std::string email;
    bool isActive = true;

    static std::vector<std::string> GetActiveCustomerNames(
      std::vector<Customer> customer);
    static std::vector<std::string> GetActiveCustomerAddresses(
      std::vector<Customer> customer);
    static std::vector<std::string> GetActiveCustomerPhoneNumbers(
```

```
            std::vector<Customer> customer);
        static std::vector<std::string> GetActiveCustomerEmails(
            std::vector<Customer> customer);

        template<typename T>
        static std::vector<T> GetActiveCustomerByFunctionField(
          std::vector<Customer> customers,
          const std::shared_ptr<BaseClass<Customer, T>>
            &classField);
    };
    #endif // __CUSTOMER_H__
```

And, the `Customer.cpp` file will be as follows:

```
    /* Customer.cpp - Step04 */
    #include "Customer.h"

    using namespace std;

    vector<string> Customer::GetActiveCustomerNames(
      vector<Customer> customers)
      {
        return Customer::GetActiveCustomerByFunctionField<string>(
        customers,
        make_shared<CustomerName>());
      }

    vector<string> Customer::GetActiveCustomerAddresses(
      vector<Customer> customer)
      {
        return Customer::GetActiveCustomerByFunctionField<string>(
          customer,
        make_shared<CustomerAddress>());
       }

    vector<string> Customer::GetActiveCustomerPhoneNumbers(
      vector<Customer> customer)
      {
        return Customer::GetActiveCustomerByFunctionField<string>(
          customer,
        make_shared<CustomerPhoneNumber>());
      }

    vector<string> Customer::GetActiveCustomerEmails(
      vector<Customer> customer)
      {
        return Customer::GetActiveCustomerByFunctionField<string>(
          customer,
```

```
    make_shared<CustomerEmail>());
  }

template<typename T>
vector<T> Customer::GetActiveCustomerByFunctionField(
  vector<Customer> customers,
  const shared_ptr<BaseClass<Customer, T>>
    &classField)
    {
      vector<T> returnList;
      for (auto &customer : customers)
      {
        if (customer.isActive)
        {
          returnList.push_back(
            classField->InvokeFunction(
            make_shared<Customer>(customer)));
        }
      }
      return returnList;
    }
```

Since the Customer class has been changed and has no registeredCustomer variable anymore, we also need to modify the RegisterCustomers() method in the main.cpp file. The previous version of the method returns nothing. Now, we will make the code return the list of customers. We also need to modify the main() method since we have to consume the new RegisterCustomers() method in the Main.cpp file. The file will contain the following block of code:

```
/* Main.cpp - Step04 */
#include <iostream>
#include "Customer.h"

using namespace std;

vector<Customer> RegisterCustomers()
{
  int i = 0;
  bool b = false;

  vector<Customer> returnValue;

  // Initialize name
  vector<string> nameList =
  {
    "William",
    "Aiden",
```

```
          "Rowan",
          "Jamie",
          "Quinn",
          "Haiden",
          "Logan",
          "Emerson",
          "Sherlyn",
          "Molly"
        };

    for (auto name : nameList)
    {
      // Create Customer object
      // and fill all properties
      Customer c;
      c.id = i++;
      c.name = name;
      c.address = "somewhere";
      c.phoneNumber = "0123";
      c.email = name + "@xyz.com";
      c.isActive = b;
      // Flip the b value
      b = !b;
      // Send data to the registeredCustomers
      returnValue.push_back(c);
    }

    return returnValue;
}

auto main() -> int
{
  cout << "[Step04]" << endl;
  cout << "--------" << endl;

  // Instance Customer object
  Customer customer;

  // Get the active customer names
  cout << "List of active customer names:" << endl;
  vector<string> activeCustomerNames =
    customer.GetActiveCustomerNames(
        RegisterCustomers());
  for (auto name : activeCustomerNames)
  {
    cout << name << endl;
  }
```

```
        return 0;
    }
```

As we can see in the preceding `main()` method, we invoke the
`GetActiveCustomerNames()` method and pass the result of the `RegisterCustomers()`
method. Now, let's try the code by running the program in the `Step06` folder. We should
get the following output on the console when we run the program:

```
Command Prompt                                          —    □    ×
[Step04]
--------
List of active customer names:
Aiden
Jamie
Haiden
Emerson
Molly
```

Again, we've got the exact same output we saw in the previous step, but with a new
approach in functional programming. Next, we will refactor the code to use a Lambda
expression to ease the filtering task.

Filtering the condition and implementing a Lambda expression

Let's focus on the `GetActiveCustomerByFunctionField()` method. There, we can find
an `if` structure to filter the active customer. As we discussed in the previous chapters, we
can use the `copy_if()` method to filter the condition. The following code snippet
implements the `copy_if()` method to filter the active customer:

```cpp
template<typename T>
vector<T> Customer::GetActiveCustomerByFunctionField(
  vector<Customer> customers,
  const shared_ptr<BaseClass<Customer, T>>
    &classField)
    {
      vector<Customer> activeCustomers;
      vector<T> returnList;

      copy_if(
        customers.begin(),
        customers.end(),
```

```
        back_inserter(activeCustomers),
        [](Customer customer)
        {
         if (customer.isActive)
            return true;
         else
            return false;
        });

        for (auto &customer : customers)
         {
            if (customer.isActive)
            {
              returnList.push_back(
              classField->InvokeFunction(
              make_shared<Customer>(customer)));
            }
         }

        return returnList;
    }
```

As we can see in the preceding code snippet, we create an anonymous method that returns true if the customer instance we pass is active. Also, we can refactor the preceding GetActiveCustomerByFunctionField() method so it will use an anonymous method again, as we can see in the following code snippet:

```
template<typename T>
vector<T> Customer::GetActiveCustomerByFunctionField(
  vector<Customer> customers,
  const shared_ptr<BaseClass<Customer, T>>
    &classField)
  {
    vector<Customer> activeCustomers;
    vector<T> returnList;

    copy_if(
      customers.begin(),
      customers.end(),
      back_inserter(activeCustomers),
      [](Customer customer)
      {
        if (customer.isActive)
          return true;
        else
          return false;
      });
```

```
        for_each(
          activeCustomers.begin(),
          activeCustomers.end(),
          [&returnList, &classField](Customer customer)
          {
            returnList.push_back(
            classField->InvokeFunction(
              make_shared<Customer>(customer))
              );
          });

      return returnList;
}
```

In addition to implementing the filtering technique using the Lambda expression, we will also add a method to the `Customer` class named `CountActiveCustomers()`. The method will count the active customers. The definition of this method should be as follows:

```
int Customer::CountActiveCustomers(
  vector<Customer> customer)
  {
    int add = 0;

    for (auto cust : customer)
    {
      // Adding 1 if the customer is active
      if(cust.isActive)
        ++add;
    }

    return add;
}
```

Now, we will have the `Customer.cpp` code in this `Step05` code block as follows:

```
/* Customer.cpp - Step05 */
#include <algorithm>
#include "Customer.h"

using namespace std;

vector<string> Customer::GetActiveCustomerNames(
  vector<Customer> customers)
  {
    return Customer::GetActiveCustomerByFunctionField<string>(
    customers,
    make_shared<CustomerName>());
  }
```

```
vector<string> Customer::GetActiveCustomerAddresses(
  vector<Customer> customer)
  {
    return Customer::GetActiveCustomerByFunctionField<string>(
      customer,
    make_shared<CustomerAddress>());
  }

vector<string> Customer::GetActiveCustomerPhoneNumbers(
  vector<Customer> customer)
  {
    return Customer::GetActiveCustomerByFunctionField<string>(
      customer,
    make_shared<CustomerPhoneNumber>());
  }

vector<string> Customer::GetActiveCustomerEmails(
  vector<Customer> customer)
  {
    return Customer::GetActiveCustomerByFunctionField<string>(
    customer,
    make_shared<CustomerEmail>());
  }

int Customer::CountActiveCustomers(
  vector<Customer> customer)
  {
    int add = 0;

    for (auto cust : customer)
    {
      // Adding 1 if the customer is active
      if(cust.isActive)
        ++add;
    }

  return add;
}

template<typename T>
vector<T> Customer::GetActiveCustomerByFunctionField(
  vector<Customer> customers,
  const shared_ptr<BaseClass<Customer, T>>
    &classField)
    {
      vector<Customer> activeCustomers;
      vector<T> returnList;
```

```
    copy_if(
      customers.begin(),
      customers.end(),
      back_inserter(activeCustomers),
     [](Customer customer)
     {
      if (customer.isActive)
          return true;
      else
          return false;
    });

    for_each(
      activeCustomers.begin(),
      activeCustomers.end(),
      [&returnList, &classField](Customer customer)
      {
        returnList.push_back(
          classField->InvokeFunction(
            make_shared<Customer>(customer))
        );
    });

    return returnList;
  }
```

Don't forget to modify the Customer.h file as well, since we have added a new method to the class. The file should contain the following piece of code:

```
/* Customer.h - Step05 */
#ifndef __CUSTOMER_H__
#define __CUSTOMER_H__

#include <string>
#include <vector>
#include <memory>

class Customer
{
  private:
    template<typename T, typename U>
    class BaseClass
    {
      public:
        virtual U InvokeFunction(
        const std::shared_ptr<T>&) = 0;
    };
```

```
class CustomerName :
  public BaseClass<Customer, std::string>
  {
    public:
      virtual std::string InvokeFunction(
        const std::shared_ptr<Customer> &customer)
        {
          return customer->name;
        }
  };

class CustomerAddress :
  public BaseClass<Customer, std::string>
  {
    public:
      virtual std::string InvokeFunction(
        const std::shared_ptr<Customer> &customer)
        {
          return customer->address;
        }
  };

class CustomerPhoneNumber :
  public BaseClass<Customer, std::string>
  {
    public:
      virtual std::string InvokeFunction(
        const std::shared_ptr<Customer> &customer)
        {
          return customer->phoneNumber;
        }
  };

class CustomerEmail :
    public BaseClass<Customer, std::string>
{
public:
    virtual std::string InvokeFunction(
        const std::shared_ptr<Customer> &customer)
    {
        return customer->email;
    }
};

public:
  int id = 0;
  std::string name;
  std::string address;
```

```
  std::string phoneNumber;
  std::string email;
  bool isActive = true;

  static std::vector<std::string> GetActiveCustomerNames(
    std::vector<Customer> customer);
  static std::vector<std::string> GetActiveCustomerAddresses(
    std::vector<Customer> customer);
  static std::vector<std::string> GetActiveCustomerPhoneNumbers(
    std::vector<Customer> customer);
  static std::vector<std::string> GetActiveCustomerEmails(
    std::vector<Customer> customer);

  static int CountActiveCustomers(
    std::vector<Customer> customer);

  template<typename T>
  static std::vector<T> GetActiveCustomerByFunctionField(
    std::vector<Customer> customers,
    const std::shared_ptr<BaseClass<Customer, T>>
        &classField);
};
#endif // __CUSTOMER_H__
```

Now, we will invoke the `CountActiveCustomers()` method in our `main()` function. We will see how we do that by examining the following `Main.cpp` code block:

```
/* Main.cpp - Step05 */
#include <iostream>
#include <chrono>
#include "Customer.h"

using namespace std;

vector<Customer> RegisterCustomers()
{
  int i = 0;
  bool b = false;

  vector<Customer> returnValue;

  // Initialize name
  vector<string> nameList =
  {
    "William",
    "Aiden",
    "Rowan",
    "Jamie",
```

```
            "Quinn",
            "Haiden",
            "Logan",
            "Emerson",
            "Sherlyn",
            "Molly"
    };

    for (auto name : nameList)
    {
        // Create Customer object
        // and fill all properties
        Customer c;
        c.id = i++;
        c.name = name;
        c.address = "somewhere";
        c.phoneNumber = "0123";
        c.email = name + "@xyz.com";
        c.isActive = b;

        // Flip the b value
        b = !b;

        // Send data to the registeredCustomers
        returnValue.push_back(c);
    }

  return returnValue;
}

auto main() -> int
{
    cout << "[Step05]" << endl;
    cout << "--------" << endl;

    // Recording start time for the program
    auto start = chrono::high_resolution_clock::now();

    // Instance Customer object
    Customer customer;

    // Counting active customers
    cout << "Total active customers: " << endl;
    cout << customer.CountActiveCustomers(
      RegisterCustomers());
    cout << endl << "--------" << endl;

    // Get the active customer names
```

```
cout << "List of active customer names:" << endl;
vector<string> activeCustomerNames =
    customer.GetActiveCustomerNames(
        RegisterCustomers());
for (auto name : activeCustomerNames)
{
    cout << name << endl;
}

// Recording end time for the program
auto finish = chrono::high_resolution_clock::now();

// Calculating the elapsed time for the program
chrono::duration<double, milli> elapsed = finish - start;

// Displaying elapsed time for the program
cout << "--------" << endl;
cout << "Total consuming time = ";
cout << elapsed.count() << " milliseconds" << endl;

return 0;
}
```

As we can see in the preceding code, we invoke the `CountActiveCustomers()` method and pass the output of the `RegisterCustomers()` method as the argument. We also add a simple stopwatch to calculate how long the code needs to run the program. The output of the preceding code should be as follows:

As we can see, we need `0.997` milliseconds to run the code in this step. However, we can optimize the preceding code to run faster by implementing recursion and memoization, which we will discuss in the next section.

Indeed, we can find out the total of the active customers by running the method of `activeCustomerNames.size()` to get the number of elements in the vector after we run the following code line:

```
vector<string> activeCustomerNames =
customer.GetActiveCustomerNames(RegisterCustomers())
```

However, the preceding code example wants to show us how the `for` loop can be transformed into recursion, to optimize the speed of execution. We will discuss this in the upcoming section.

Implementing recursion and memoization techniques to the Customer class

If we look at the `CountActiveCustomers()` method definition in `Step05`, we use the `for` loop to count the active customers. However, we can rewrite the method to use the recursion technique. Let's take a look at the following code, which is the new definition for the `CountActiveCustomers()` method:

```
int Customer::CountActiveCustomers(
  vector<Customer> customer)
  {
    if(customer.empty())
      return 0;
    else
    {
      // Adding 1 if the customer is active
      int add = customer.front().isActive ? 1 : 0;

      // Removing the first element of vector
      // It's similar with removing head
      // and pass the tail
      customer.erase(customer.begin());

      // Running the recursion
      return add + CountActiveCustomers(
        customer);
    }
  }
```

As we can see in the preceding code snippet, we use tail recursion for the `CountActiveCustomers()` method. We just need to increment the `add` variable every time we find an active customer in the `customer` vector. The code then removes the first element of the `customer` vector and passes it to the `CountActiveCustomers()` method again. We recurse this process until the element of the `customer` vector is empty.

Also, we use the `Memoization` class we discussed in `Chapter 5`, *Procrastinating the Execution Process Using Lazy Evaluation*, to optimize our code. We will modify the `main()` function in the `Main.cpp` file so the `main()` function contains the following code snippet:

```cpp
auto main() -> int
{
    cout << "[Step06]" << endl;
    cout << "--------" << endl;

    // Recording start time for the program
    auto start = chrono::high_resolution_clock::now();

    // Instance Customer object
    Customer customer;

    // Counting active customers
    cout << "Total active customers: " << endl;
    cout << customer.CountActiveCustomers(
        RegisterCustomers());
    cout << endl << "--------" << endl;

    // Initializing memoization instance
    Memoization<vector<string>> custMemo(
        [customer]()
        {
            return customer.GetActiveCustomerNames(
                RegisterCustomers());
        });

    // Get the active customer names
    cout << "List of active customer names:" << endl;
    vector<string> activeCustomerNames =
        custMemo.Fetch();
    for (auto name : activeCustomerNames)
    {
        cout << name << endl;
    }

    // Recording end time for the program
    auto finish = chrono::high_resolution_clock::now();
```

```
        // Calculating the elapsed time for the program
        chrono::duration<double, milli> elapsed = finish - start;

        // Displaying elapsed time for the program
        cout << "--------" << endl;
        cout << "Total consuming time = ";
        cout << elapsed.count() << " milliseconds" << endl;

        return 0;
    }
```

As we can see in the preceding code snippet, we now run the
`GetActiveCustomerNames()` method from the `Memoization` instance by calling the
`Fetch()` method. If we run the `Step06` code, we should see the following output on the
console:

```
[Step06]
--------
Total active customers:
5
--------
List of active customer names:
Aiden
Jamie
Haiden
Emerson
Molly
--------
Total consuming time = 0.502 milliseconds
```

The code now only needs `0.502` milliseconds to run. Compared to the `Step05` code, the
speed of code execution is almost twice as fast. It proves that, by using the functional
approach, we can gain not only a better code structure, but also speed optimization.

Debugging the code

Sometimes, in the coding process, when we run the code, we've got an unexpected result
from one or more variables. It might happen in the middle of the execution. To avoid
getting stuck in this situation, we can analyze our program by running it step-by-step. We
can use the debugger tool that is included in the GCC compiler--**GDB (The GNU Project
Debugger)**. This tool allows us to figure out what happens inside the target program while
it executes, or what it was doing at the moment it crashed. In this section, we will apply the
GDB to ease our programming task and find a solution for the problem and deal with it.

Starting the debugging tool

Now, let's prepare the executable file we will analyze. We will use the code from the `Step01` folder since it's a simple code, and we can learn easily from it. We have to recompile the code using the `-g` option and name the executable as `customer.exe`. The following are the three commands to compile the code so it can be debugged:

```
g++ -Wall -g -c Main.cpp -o Main.o
g++ -Wall -g -c Customer.cpp -o Customer.o
g++ Main.o Customer.o -o Customer.exe
```

> GDB can only analyze the executable file that contains the debugging information and symbols that are important in the debugging process. We can insert the `-g` option when we compile the source so the debugging information and symbol will be added to the executable file.

Typing `gdb customer` on the console will open the debugger tool and load the debugger information and symbol from the `customer.exe` file. We will then see the following screenshot on the console:

```
Command Prompt - gdb customer                                  —    □    ×

E:\Debugging>gdb customer
GNU gdb (GDB) 8.0
Copyright (C) 2017 Free Software Foundation, Inc.
License GPLv3+: GNU GPL version 3 or later <http://gnu.org/licenses/gpl.html>
This is free software: you are free to change and redistribute it.
There is NO WARRANTY, to the extent permitted by law.  Type "show copying"
and "show warranty" for details.
This GDB was configured as "x86_64-w64-mingw32".
Type "show configuration" for configuration details.
For bug reporting instructions, please see:
<http://www.gnu.org/software/gdb/bugs/>.
Find the GDB manual and other documentation resources online at:
<http://www.gnu.org/software/gdb/documentation/>.
For help, type "help".
Type "apropos word" to search for commands related to "word"...
Reading symbols from customer...done.
(gdb)
```

As we can see in the preceding screenshot, it has successfully read the symbol from the `customer.exe` file. Then, type `start` in the GDB console to start the analyzing process. The debugger will create a temporary breakpoint in the first line of the `main()` method. We will see the following screenshot on the console after starting the GDB:

```
Command Prompt - gdb customer                           —   □   ×
(gdb) start
Temporary breakpoint 1 at 0x401b81: file Main.cpp, line 52.
Starting program: E:\Debugging\customer.exe
[New Thread 16716.0x12f4]
[New Thread 16716.0x2bd8]
warning: Can not parse XML library list; XML support was disabled at compile ti
me

Thread 1 hit Temporary breakpoint 1, main () at Main.cpp:52
52              cout << "[Step01]" << endl;
(gdb)
```

Now, the program is in the debugging process. We can continue the process to analyze what is going on with the program. In the next section, we can choose between continuing step by step or running the program until the next breakpoint is found.

 To start the debugging process, we can either call the `run` or `start` command. The former will start our program under GDB, while the latter will behave similarly but will execute the code line by line. The difference is, if we don't have the breakpoint yet, the program will run as usual, just like it does when we call the `run` command, while the debugger will automatically set the breakpoint in the main block of code and the program will stop when it reaches that breakpoint, if we start with the `start` command.

Continuing and stepping the debugging process

There are three commands to continue the step in the preceding section. They are as follows:

- `continue`: This resumes the execution of the program until our program completes normally. If it finds a breakpoint, the execution will stop at the line where the breakpoint is set.

- `step`: This executes just one more step of our program. The step might mean either one line of source code or one machine instruction. If it finds the invocation of a function, it will come into the function and run one more step inside the function.
- `next`: This continues to the next line in the current stack frame. In other words, if the next command finds the invocation of a function, it will not enter the function.

Since we haven't set the breakpoint yet, let's type the `next` command so the debugging pointer goes to the next line of the code. We will run the `next` command multiple times until the end of the code is reached (or until we can see that the process is exited normally). We should see the following screenshot when we apply the `next` command multiple times:

```
Command Prompt - gdb  customer                                    —    □    ✕
66              for (auto &name : activeCustomerNames)
(gdb)
71              return 0;
(gdb)
65                  customer.GetActiveCustomerNames();
(gdb)
60              Customer customer;
(gdb)
72      }
(gdb)
0x00000000004013f7 in __tmainCRTStartup ()
(gdb)
Single stepping until exit from function __tmainCRTStartup,
which has no line number information.
[Thread 16716.0x2bd8 exited with code 0]
[Inferior 1 (process 16716) exited normally]
(gdb)
```

As we can see in the preceding screenshot, we can analyze our program by running it step by step. Next, we will set the breakpoint if we have a suspect object to be analyzed.

 We just need to press the Enter key to run the previous command in GDB. Pressing the Q key will make the debugging console exit to the window console.

Setting and deleting the breakpoint

Let's exit from the debugging console by typing the *Q* key. We need to restart the debugging, so we need to type `gdb customer` again on the window console. After that, instead of typing the `start` command, let's set the breakpoint before we continue the process. Let's type `break 68` and `break Customer.cpp:15` respectively in the GDB console. The output is shown as follows:

```
Command Prompt - gdb customer                                    —    □

(gdb) break 68
Breakpoint 1 at 0x401c54: file Main.cpp, line 68.
(gdb) break Customer.cpp:15
Breakpoint 2 at 0x401dcd: file Customer.cpp, line 15.
(gdb)
```

Now, we have two breakpoint in separate files--`Main.cpp` and `Customer.cpp`. We can now start the debugger by typing `run` in GDB console, as we can see in the following screenshot:

```
Command Prompt - gdb customer                                    —    □

(gdb) run
Starting program: E:\Debugging\customer.exe
[New Thread 12960.0x3784]
[New Thread 12960.0xdfc]
warning: Can not parse XML library list; XML support was disabled at compile t
me
[Step01]
--------
List of active customer names:

Thread 1 hit Breakpoint 2, Customer::GetActiveCustomerNames[abi:cxx11]() (
    this=0x76fda0) at Customer.cpp:15
15                  returnList.push_back(customer.name);
(gdb)
```

Since the debugger hit the `GetActiveCustomerNames()` method first, it stops in the line where we put the breakpoint in that method, which is line `15` in the `Customer.cpp` file. Just type the `continue` command and press *Enter* multiple times until it hits the breakpoint in the `Main.cpp` file, line `69`.

Printing the object value

Let's rerun the debugger by setting the breakpoint on line `68` in the `Main.cpp` file, then start the debugger until it hits the breakpoint. After the breakpoint is hit, type `print name` to see what the value of the name variable is. The following screenshot shows the steps of the process:

```
Command Prompt - gdb customer                                     —  □  ✕

(gdb) break 68
Breakpoint 1 at 0x401c54: file Main.cpp, line 68.
(gdb) run
Starting program: E:\Debugging\customer.exe
[New Thread 2400.0x9dc]
warning: Can not parse XML library list; XML support was disabled at compile ti
me
[New Thread 2400.0x2634]
[Step01]
--------
List of active customer names:

Thread 1 hit Breakpoint 1, main () at Main.cpp:68
68                  cout << name << endl;
(gdb) print name
$1 = (std::__cxx11::basic_string<char, std::char_traits<char>, std::allocator<c
har> > &) @0x193bd0: {static npos = 18446744073709551615,
  _M_dataplus = {<std::allocator<char>> = {<__gnu_cxx::new_allocator<char>> = {
<No data fields>}, <No data fields>}, _M_p = 0x193be0 "Aiden"},
  _M_string_length = 5, {_M_local_buf = "Aiden\000-º\rd-º\rd-º",
    _M_allocated_capacity = 13451408136173021505}}
(gdb)                                              The value of "name" variable
```

As we can see in the preceding screenshot, the value of the `name` variable is `Aiden`. We can continue the debugging by typing the `continue` command so the debugger hits the breakpoint again in the `for` loop, then typing `print name` to find out the next name value.

There are so many commands in the GDB that, will be overloaded if they are written in this book. If you need to find more commands in the GDB, refer to the following link:

```
https://www.gnu.org/software/gdb/documentation/
```

Summary

In the last chapter of this book, we developed the functional class successfully by refactoring it from the imperative class that we can use to create a more complex program with. We implemented what we learned in the previous chapters. We also discussed the debugging technique, which is a useful weapon when we face an unexpected result or get a crash in the middle of the program.

Index

www.ingramcontent.com/pod-product-compliance
Lightning Source LLC
Chambersburg PA
CBHW080627060326
40690CB00021B/4844